NORTHERN IRELAND

Edited by Jonathan Bartlett

THE REFERENCE SHELF

Volume 54 Number 6

The H. W. Wilson Company

New York   1983

THE REFERENCE SHELF

The books in this series contain reprints of articles, excerpts from books, and addresses on current issues and social trends in the United States and other countries. There are six separately bound numbers in each volume, all of which are generally published in the same calendar year. One number is a collection of recent speeches; each of the others is devoted to a single subject and gives background information and discussion from various points of view, concluding with a comprehensive bibliography. Books in the series may be purchased individually or on subscription.

Library of Congress Cataloging in Publication Data

Main entry under title:

Northern Ireland.

   (Reference shelf ; v. 54, no. 6)
   Bibliography: p.
   1. Northern Ireland--History--1969-   --Addresses, essays, lectures. 2. Northern Ireland--Social conditions--Addresses, essays, lectures. 3. Maze Prison (Lisburn, Northern Ireland)--Addresses, essays, lectures. I. Bartlett, Jonathan. II. Series.
DA990.U46N665 1983   941.60824   82-23876
ISBN 0-8242-0670-3

International Standard Book Number 0-8242-0670-3

Printed in the United States of America

CONTENTS

PREFACE

"Come away, O human child," wrote the poet William Butler Yeats at the end of the last century, "for the world's more full of weeping than you can understand." And it seems that in respect to the poet's native Ireland, at least, there is, has been, and bids fair to continue to be more weeping than the ordinary human mind can possibly comprehend. The cause of all this weeping is a complicated historic dispute between the Irish and the English generally referred to as the Troubles in Ireland and as the Irish Question by the international diplomatic community. (A "question" in diplomatic language refers to a problem so complicated and intractable that no logical outcome seems possible.) One aspect of the Troubles is that its roots are so deeply embedded in the past that attitudes on both sides are incomprehensible without at least a brief glance at Anglo-Irish relations over not just the years, but the centuries.

During the 1960s, a team of gentle English satirists inserted in one of their songs a reference to the Irish, about whom they said, "they blow up policemen, or so I have heard, and blame it on Cromwell and William the Third." Lightly amusing, innocuous, indeed accurate in a certain sense, but to the Irish utterly infuriating. To the Irish locked into their ancestral struggle, one does not mock the past. It is the past, after all, that gives legitimacy to the bloodshed and sorrow of the present. Indeed, where else could the singing of "The Boyne Water" cause Catholics (Ulstermen and others alike) to look around for the nearest rock to heave at the singer's head? The song commemorates a battle fought in 1690 pitting the Catholic Irish against the forces of England's Protestant King William III and won by the latter. It is placed, in Irish minds, in the same category as the genocidal invasion some fifty years earlier by Oliver Cromwell. When hostilities have been going on as long as this, no wonder the Irish are not amused.

Relations between the Irish and the English have remained strained down through all these years, ranging from surliness and ill grace to pitched battles and virtually total war. In the 1920s, the southern section of Ireland, plus three of the nine northern countries that comprise what was known as Ulster, were spun off, ultimately to form what is today the Republic of Ireland. The six remaining northern counties remained part of Great Britain, retaining the name Ulster. The Irish Question today is essentially that of Ulster. Predominantly Protestant, the population of Ulster is deeply suspicious of its southern neighbor, fearful that unification would put an end to its religion, its way of life, perhaps to life itself. The Nationalists, those who want to see all Ireland unified, object to the way Catholics are treated in Ulster and insist merger is inevitable anyway. Differences of opinion have degenerated into violence on both sides. The Irish Republican Army, a volunteer non-governmental organization in the south, attempted to pressure the North to achieve unification. Eventually an offshoot of the IRA, called the Provisional Wing, stepped up the violence to the point of terrorism. Countering the Provisionals —the "Provos"—were Ulster terrorists waging their own battle against Catholics in the North, and the British Army, which had come into the dispute originally as peace keepers at the request of the government of Ulster. Against this background of blood and weeping, the Irish Question continues on its vexing way.

Section I of this compilation gives the historical background of the Troubles and some of the more recent manifestations of Anglo-Irish hostility. Section II focuses on a remarkable phenomenon—a series of highly publicized hunger strikes by IRA militants captured by the British and placed in a British jail in Ulster. Section III deals with how ordinary citizens are coping with life and politics in embattled Belfast, Ulster's capital. And Section IV presents some thoughts on whether, and if so how, there might be some resolution to the whole ghastly mess.

The Editor particularly wishes to thank the authors and publishers who have granted permission to reprint the materials that make up this compilation. Special thanks are also due to the staff of the New York City Public Library System and especially to the reference division of the Nyack (N.Y.) Public Library.

Jonathan Bartlett

October, 1982

I. BACKGROUND TO WEEPING

EDITOR'S INTRODUCTION

The past has always been an extremely important factor in Irish affairs, to the point where one recent student of troubled Ulster found written on a Belfast wall the following lines:

To Hell with the future and long live the past.
May God in His heaven look down on Belfast.

As with all of us, however, the past the Irish like to evoke is not always exactly the past as it was. Sometimes it is the past as they like to remember it. For example, as Constantine FitzGibbon, the Irish-American novelist and historian and the author of the first selection, has pointed out elsewhere, the victory that sealed the rule of William III over Ireland was not in fact the battle at the Boyne River, successful though he had been there. The decisive victory actually took place a year later at Aughrim, where the Catholic forces were totally routed. However, Aughrim is in the province of Connaught, not Ulster, and it is perfectly understandable that the Protestant Ulstermen would prefer to commemorate a battle on their own soil rather than that of a neighbor—and a Catholic neighbor at that.

The purpose of the first selection—which comprises the first three chapters of Mr. FitzGibbon's book *Red Hand: The Ulster Colony* —is to give some sense of the history that lies within the marrow of every Irishman's bones. In the course of it, several terms will occur used in an unfamiliar way. First is the Pale, referring to an area of land (its size varied over the years) generally centered around Dublin, This area, unlike the rest of Ireland, was ruled directly by England and was subject to the laws of Parliament. Once England took sovereignty over the rest of Ireland, the term was no longer of any use and was dropped. Another term is Plantation, or Plantation of Ulster. This simply describes the policy of sending colonists to Ulster where they were settled or "planted." Even though the Plantation dated from the first decade of the 1600s, the descendants of the original settlers are often looked upon and resented by some of the more extreme Catholics as outsiders and invaders and one of the root causes in the continuation of the Troubles.

So much for Anglo-Irish relations over the centuries. The second selection reflects the history and controversy from a different viewpoint of more recent years. Reprinted from *Commentary* , it is the work of Herb Greer, an American writer who has spent much of his life in Britain and continental Europe.

RED HAND: THE ULSTER COLONY[1]

1. Ulster's Origins

Throughout most of the middle ages, and particularly during the sixteenth century, Ulster was the heartland of Irish resistance to Anglo-Saxon dominance; perhaps the heartland of the whole 'Celtic' world which stretched along the Atlantic seaboard from southern Brittany to the northernmost isles of Scotland. Until the Irish Elizabethan Wars spread to that province (1596-1603) Ulster had never been really conquered, though it had been raided by Vikings, Normans and Scots and there was, indeed, already a Scots-Irish 'colony' along its eastern seaboard, in what are now the counties Antrim and Down. The Anglo-Normans had overrun almost all of southern and western Ireland, and though they had rapidly been assimilated—had become 'more Irish than the Irish'—they had brought with them a measure of continental modes, of that feudal attitude which, deriving indirectly from Rome, was to lead ultimately to the world of the Renaissance and thus to modern society: primogeniture, that is to say the family rather than the tribe as basic unit of the human community: from

[1] Book by Constantine FitzGibbon. Chapters 1, 2, and 3. Doubleday & Co., Garden City, New York, 1971. Copyright © 1971 by Constantine FitzGibbon. Reprinted by permission of Doubleday & Company, Inc.

this, a firm concept of property and particularly of land as property: a vague heritage of Roman law: and the concept of a centralized government. In Leinster, particularly in the Pale, these ideas took root. In Munster and Connaught they faded among Irish mists, but the memory lingered on among Gaelic-speaking Fitzgeralds and de Burgoes and the other great families of Norman descent. In Ulster, until the Plantation, they were for all intents and purposes unknown. There the ancient laws and customs of the Irish still prevailed over almost all of what later became the Nine Counties, except for the Scots communities, and when it came to fighting the foreigners formidable reinforcements, in the form of mercenaries called 'gallowglasses', could be recruited from the Scottish Highlands and islands. It was there that the greatest and last act of Gaelic rebellion against alien rule and alien ways took place, led by Hugh O'Neill, Ulster's principal chieftain and, briefly, the real King of Ireland. Descended from Niall of the Nine Hostages, High King of Ireland from 380 to 405, his tribal emblem was the Red Hand which in due course became and has remained the emblem of all Ulster. His attempt to defend, by force of arms, his people's ancient customs and lands, rebellion in English eyes, failed, at last, utterly. O'Neill was forced to flee overseas and died in Rome. His province was in ruins, and most of his people dead. The government in London then moved in, to ensure that such a dangerous rebellion should never happen again. Ulster was planted.

The political and military aspects of the Anglo-Irish wars of the late sixteenth and early seventeenth centuries had quite rapidly polarized about religion. When these wars began the Reformation, in England, was far from complete and still subject to reversion: for purposes of policy Queen Elizabeth I was quite capable of following a more subtle policy than her late sister's and restoring, as their father Henry VIII had wished to do, something like an eotype of the later French 'Gallican' Church. By the time these wars were over events in the Low Countries, the almost perpetual threat of a Spanish invasion with consequent, similar anti-Protestant atrocities in England, and finally the Gunpowder Plot of 1605 had hardened the English into an anti-papist ideology that was to endure for two centuries and more. In Ireland, on the other hand, the process had been precisely reversed. When the Elizabethan wars started religion in Ireland had reached a low point perhaps without precedent before, and certainly since. The old mediaeval Church had declined, at least as much as it had done in England before the Reformation, into a useless, expensive and largely irreligious social organization. Apart from the work of the Franciscan friars it provided little, if any, spiritual leadership for the people: divorce and concubinage were commonplace and brigandage almost an accepted way of life, at least outside the Viking-founded and now partly anglicized coastal cities. When, under the early Tudor monarchs, Church lands and Church property were seized and sold few who were not clerics either objected or were even surprised. However, in Ireland there were virtually no Protestant pastors to replace the Roman Catholic priests. Anglican divines might accept one benefice, or more frequently several, but seldom bothered to visit all their parishes. Ireland was reverting, rapidly, to paganism. The wars both accelerated this relapse into savagery but simultaneously changed, and drastically, the religious attitude of the people.

Ireland and Holland were at this period the two major battlefields of the massive counter-offensive launched by the Counter-Reformation, soon to be extended into the German Thirty Years' War. Master-minded from Rome and using the might of Spain as its first and principal weapon, this counter-offensive employed as its agents very clever and very brave missionary priests, of whom the most famous were Loyola's new Order of Jesus, and its major emotional-political lever the devotion of those who preferred the Old Faith to the New. In Ireland the priests were extremely effective and regained the respect that had been lost in past generations, while the English enemy became increasingly the Protestant enemy. And when the wars were lost, and the Irish leaders had fled abroad, been killed or reduced to impotence in their own divided territories, after acceptance of English law and an oath of allegiance to the English monarch, it was inevitably to these brave, competent, outlawed priests that the Irish looked for leadership. They were to do so for several centuries, and the tradition lingers on even today, for even today the Thirty Years' War is still being fought in the streets of Belfast.

Thus by the time of the Plantation of Ulster an Anglo-Irish War, now over, had become a Catholic-Protestant confrontation. Therefore when the English government decided to plant Ulster, this could only be a Protestant plantation, to keep down and if possible expel the Roman Catholic 'natives', those dangerous, savage people who had so nearly opened Ireland, and through Ireland England, to be ultimate horrors of Spanish conquest: the English governing class was only too well aware of what Alva had done in the Low Countries.

The whole apparatus of English administration was then imposed upon Ulster, an apparatus infinitely more sophisticated than the old Irish system, complete as it was counties, shires, sheriffs, the English legal system, the Protestant religion and so on. This in itself, though bewildering to many of the Irish and distasteful to many if not most of the people's temporal and spiritual leaders, was not unacceptable to all. The famished survivors of the terrible war were, as always and everywhere, anxious to see a revival of order, and in such circumstances even an alien order is better than none: nor can the mass of the people have particularly relished the traditional feuding and raiding and raping by the petty chieftains who had ruled their lives for centuries. In such circumstances the peace even of the grave is better than no peace at all. In our own times it was so in Germany in 1945, it will be so in Vietnam tomorrow, and it was so in Ulster in 1604. But then the English began to steal the land, using English legal methods in the province.

2. British Colonization and Religious Polarization

After the soldiers always come the carpet-baggers. Nowhere was this more true than in Ulster after 1603. The English general, Mountjoy, had a very wise respect and, it would seem, even a measure of personal affection for The O'Neill and for his principal lieutenant or ally, the head of the O'Donnells whose land lay to his west. The terms of the surrender were generous. The Irish chieftains were regranted most of their lands, after swearing allegiance to the Crown. This however turned them into feudal lords rather than Irish chieftains, and the change caused immense confusion among their people. As The O'Neill, Hugh had been the local king or *ri*, but had not personally owned any land, for the land belonged to all his people when it did not belong to the peoples of his allies and client kinglets. There were, indeed no real borders. Since virtually the entire economy of inland Ulster had hitherto been based upon the cow and since the population was almost semi-nomadic in its search for pasturage among the great forests that then covered most of the land, this had led to brigandage, cattle-rustling and petty local wars—a situation not dissimilar to that of the American West as it was opened up in the nineteenth century, where many of the toughest, earliest settlers were, as it happened, the descendants of Ulster Scots-Irishmen.

Once The O'Neill had finally accepted the royal jurisdiction that he was now the Earl of Tyrone, all this changed. The land now belonged to him and should pass to his oldest son or nearest male relative on his death, rather than to the most suitable O'Neill within a reasonably close degree of co-sanguinuity. This meant in effect that what the Ulster chieftains were surrendering to the English was not their own to give away. True, feudal land tenure had long taken root in other parts of the island, particularly in Leinster and in large parts of Munster, but even in those provinces the great Anglo-Norman families, while preserving the principal of primogeniture, had in greater or lesser measure reverted to the sort of primitive communism of co-ownership that had prevailed over all Europe before the Roman conquest and its feudal successor states. . . .

Thus O'Neill's surrender was in essence a betrayal of his people and of Gaellic civilization in that civilization's heartland. Red Hugh O'Donnell must have realized this at once, for he fled abroad where he soon died, probably from poison given to him by an English secret agent. O'Neill tried to retain his position, but with the departure of his old enemy-friend, Mountjoy, in 1606 and the increasing pressure of the carpet-baggers, who had London's full support, he realized that without the support of his people he had no longer any role to play in his native land. In 1607 he, with Rory O'Donnell and close on a hundred of the most important persons in Ulster, quietly boarded a ship in Lough Swilly and sailed to the continent, never to return.

It is generally agreed that 'the flight of the earls' marks the real end of Gaelic civilization as a political entity, though as a cultural and even as a social phenomenon the tradition lingered on and flickers still, while Irish patriotism was of course constantly to be revived in a variety of forms and behind a multitude of slogans.

For centuries it was English policy to make Ireland 'pay for itself', that is to say to pay for supporting the English standing army which was there to prevent rebellion and—when rebellion occurred as it had always done and was to do with remarkable regularity almost once per generation—to pay for the cost of subduing the rebellion. In the Ireland of the sixteenth, seventeenth and eighteenth centuries there was virtually no industry or commerce that could be successfully milked, as was to happen in the nineteenth and twentieth, and the only wealth that the English could draw on in Ireland was land. Since land is obviously not transportable, the only way the English could transfer it into cash was to seize it and sell it. This was the primary, economic basis of British colonialism, and remained so until the end of the British empire. From a socio-political point of view this policy of land seizure hid a secondary motive. The purchasers and new landlords were intended to be English or Scots so far as possible. They would bring with them English ways, the English language, English law and the English or Scots versions of the Protestant religion. Since for centuries the English, like their cousins in Germany and their descendants in America, have generally regarded their own methods as being divinely inspired, such a substitution of cultural and spiritual values to replace the benighted ideas and ideals of the ignorant natives could only be, in English eyes, of positive benefit to all, from Drogheda to Delhi. Such was the ideological justification of conquest and plunder. It was later to assume slightly more sophisticated forms of reference, such as the imposition of an incorruptible civil service on the Malayans or Ghanaians, but in Ulster, in the first half of the seventeenth century, the motives behind the Plantation were crude: to make money, to keep the Irish down, and if possible to turn them into second-class Englishmen or Scots or at least to prevent them from speaking, thinking and thus even being Irish.

The Plantation, that first deliberate plantation, of Ulster was very far from being homogeneous. The most easterly counties, Antrim and the northern part of the County Down, already had a largely Scots population. Indeed the sea is there so narrow that the distinction between Scots and Irish was and is almost irrelevant. By the mid-sixteenth century there had been a large Scottish 'colony' in Antrim, the MacDonnells. (The present head of this clan, Lord Antrim, still has his seat at Glenarm and is chairman of the independent television service called Ulster Television.) These areas were therefore not ripe for expropriation and colonization. An attempt to plant northeastern Ulster in the 1570s had failed: the colonists had either sold up and gone home or had married Irishwomen and produced Irish, and Irish-speaking, children as had happened over the centuries in Munster and Connaught. Only in Leinster, and only in parts of that province, had the English *geist* taken firm root. It was therefore to the hinterland that the colonists and the carpetbaggers had to look. They came, they saw, they stole what the soldiers had conquered. Their method was really quite simple.

The province of Ulster consisted in 1607, as it does today, of nine counties. (That part of the United Kingdom usually referred to as 'Northern Ireland', though it does not include the extreme north of the island, contains six of these counties.) Of the nine, two were not meet for plantation: Antrim and Down already contained large Scottish and smaller English settlements, and since after 1603 England was to be ruled by a Scots dynasty for almost all of eighty-seven years, these people were in theory loyal subjects of the London government—which indeed they usually were—and their land was therefore not expropriated. The large estate called Clandeboye in North Down, the property of Con O'Neill, a member of that great family and consisting of some 60,000 acres that include what was then the village of Belfast, was divided into three. One share went to a keen and efficient Scottish colonist from Ayrshire called Hugh Montgomery, one third, apparently as a reward, to another Scot named James Hamilton who had usefully served the Crown for many years as a secret agent in Dublin; the final portion Con O'Neill was allowed to keep, but within a very few years his new Scots neighbors had, by legal and commercial methods, acquired almost all of his land too. With such people active in Down, and the MacDonnells across Belfast Lough with the utterly loyal settlement at Carrickfergus, there was no need to plant the two eastern counties.

In the southeastern part of the province the small county of Monaghan had already been expropriated in Elizabethan times. This was MacMahon country and when Hugh MacMahon was attainted and executed for collecting his rents by a customary Irish method—that is to say the seizure of cattle—the county was broken up and feudalized in the 1590s. Seven MacMahons and a MacKenna were allotted between two and five thousand acres apiece: they were entitled to demand £10 per 960 acres from each of their tenants: and from this they had to pay a quit rent to the Crown, represented by a Seneschal. This was a comparatively successful implementation of the policy of 'surrender and re-grant' that Queen Elizabeth had inherited from her father, Henry VIII, who had first formulated it in 1541. Its intention was the destruction of the ancient Irish social structure. By 1608 in Monaghan there was no longer 'a MacMahon' but seven great landowners with that name and often at loggerheads one with another. Therefore Monaghan, like Antrim and Down, was not planted. To do so would only have disrupted those long range plans for the substitution of English for Irish methods in social arrangements which it was the English colonialists' intention to enforce. Monaghan, in fact, reverted quite quickly to Irish ways. Together with Donegal and Cavan it is one of the three counties of Ulster that are now part of the Republic of Ireland.

The other six counties of Ulster (Donegal, Coleraine, soon to be renamed Londonderry, Tyrone, Fermanagh, Cavan, Armagh) were to be planted. The first was Cavan in 1605, even before the flight of the earls: the other five in 1608, immediately after that event. And here it is necessary to explain the whole method and motive of 'plantation', in Ireland as in Virginia and elsewhere, which was the main method of early English colonialism.

The basic motive of the plantations—for even in Ulster we must speak of many, carried out over many years—was not, or at least not consciously on the part of the newcomers, the destruction of Gaelic culture nor even in the first instance of the Roman Catholic religion. True, since the Statute of Kilkenny in 1366, the English had made periodic attempts to stamp out the Irish language in the areas they controlled, principally in the Pale of Dublin, and to compel the subject people to dress as Englishmen. These measures were, however, directed more against the Anglo-Norman settlers of the original conquest and their successors, known as the Old English, who were likewise becoming assimilated amidst the native population, rather than against the Irish themselves. In Ulster in the early seventeenth century the Anglo-Normans, small in numbers in any event, were almost completely Gaelicized, and the Old English were also rare. Though the operation was not directed against Irish culture as such at this time—this was to come later—it was directed against the old Irish legal system (the Brehon Laws, which had almost nothing in common with Roman Law), against the Irish economy, which was to be expropriated, and against the Irish people, who were to be in as large a measure as possible expelled to make way for the planters or reduced to the level of second-class citizens.

As early as the reign of Queen Mary, in the 1550s, an attempt to extend the Pale westwards by planting Leix and Offaly with loyal Old English had soon failed, as usual owing to assimilation. (Curiously, the counties, renamed Queen's and King's counties, were allowed to retain their new names throughout centuries of Protestant domination and re-conquest: it was left to the Irish Free State to abolish this memorial to his Most Catholic Majesty, King Philip of Spain, and to his wife, the last Roman Catholic queen to reign over England and Ireland.) An attempt at a plantation in northern Ulster in the 1570s had similarly failed. The plantation of Munster was carried out in far more systematic fashion between the two Desmond revolts and after the final suppression of the second in 1583. This is hardly surprising since the men in charge in London were the two most powerful men in the English government, Burleigh and Walsingham, while the men on the spot included Sir Walter Raleigh and his half-brother Sir Humphrey Gilbert. Sir Humphrey had not only been governor of Munster twenty years before but was to plant the first British colony on the American continent. Sir Walter Raleigh's career as one of the first and perhaps among the greatest English colonists in the New World is common knowledge. It is important to realize that these tough Elizabethan politicians and soldiers regarded the colonization of Munster in exactly the same light, and from the same point of view, as they regarded the colonization of the eastern seaboard of America: it was wealth that they were after, the wealth of the natives. In this they were merely copying—at that time unsuccessfully—their Spanish enemies, with the general backing of Queen Elizabeth and her ministers.

The planting of Queen's and King's counties was not a success. 'Undertakers' were appointed, who became tenants-in-chief to the Crown on the understanding that they import English sub-tenants. The businessmen found it easier and more profitable to let the land to Irishmen, so nothing was changed save that land-tenure was made to approximate to the English pattern, while the authority of the Crown, in theory at least, was strengthened. Even these English gains were in large measure swept away in the wars. At about the same time a more successful, at least temporarily successful, attempt was made to bring the province to Connaught into the English system, this time without conquest. The so-called Composition of Connaught introduced money rents and English land-titles instead of the prevailing confusion of Gaelic and feudal tenures. This too was to be swept away, though again only temporarily, in the next Anglo-Irish war. The precedents were being slowly and steadily established, but at no profit to the Crown and, indeed, at great expense as army after English army had to be despatched across the Irish Sea only to melt away, more usually of disease or hunger than in battle, in the fearsome, trackless forests or in isolated outposts. Colonies were supposed to pay their way, at least, and were intended to bring in a profit. Ireland was doing neither, and Ulster least of all. Therefore when the Great O'Neill's rebellion was finally crushed, and the earls had flown, and Sir Cahir O'Doherty's rebellion of 1608—in the course of which he burned Derry—had been crushed and the Irish chieftain killed on Tory Island, it was decided in London that more Draconian, more up-to-date, more efficient and above all more lucrative methods must be employed in the plantations of the devastated, starving counties of Ulster.

One of the most intractable problems of Elizabeth's and James I's Irish operations had been the payment and victualling of the soldiers. The English army at that time was remarkably corrupt at almost all levels. The contractors and sub-contractors stole and sold supplies of food, and even of weapons, intended for the men in the remote fastnesses of Ireland, all the way from Bristol or even from London as the carts creaked along the roads and tracks to Coleraine or Kerry. The officers stole the money with which the troops were supposed to be paid. In vast numbers the penniless, starving soldiers deserted when there was nothing left to loot from the natives, and often there had been nothing for a long, long time. The entire army's pay was almost always in arrears. And neither Queen Elizabeth's nor James I's ministers were anxious to have these 'sturdy beggars' back in England, not so much for fear of those anti-social methods of self-help which they had inevitably learned in the Irish wars but rather because an unemployed military rabble was in itself a highly undesirable component in a fragile, insecure society that was becoming increasingly divided as bitterness steadily increased over religious and parliamentary matters. Therefore, instead of pay, it was decided to plant approximately one-third of the sequestrated land of Ulster with discharged soldiers. No doubt among the clever and educated renaissance men in London and Dublin there were also memories from Oxford and Cambridge—and the brand new Trinity College, Dublin—of Roman methods of colonization, of discharged legionaries keeping Colchester or Trier quiet by their mere presence. It seemed a good financial and political solution. It failed, at first, because the majority of the planted soldiery either became Irishmen, in at least one generation, or sold up to the undertakers or even to the Irish and went home.

The second class of persons who received land-grants were the so-called 'servitors'. They were Irishmen who had in some measure or other proved their loyalty to the Crown in the recent wars. In view of the constant changing of sides for so many years, it must have been even more difficult in Ireland in 1608 to decide who had been a 'servitor' than it was in Germany in 1945 to decide who had been ant anti-Nazi. In view of the countryman's entirely comprehensible passion for land, his own people's land, in a country that offered no other form of wealth and survival for himself and his people, one does not need to be a psychologist in order to be quite sure that many of these 'servitors' hated the English expropriators, and we know that many of their sort took part in Owen Roe O'Neill's rebellion of 1642.

The third portion of confiscated Irish land—and precise percentages of course varied from district to district and from time to time—was sold to the 'undertakers' to help recoup the Crown for the cost of the wars and to pay for the government of this part of the Irish colony. They were more carefully supervised than they had been in Munster, but though a great deal of this land passed into English or more often Lowland Scots hands, much of it passed only to be resold into Irish hands as the province quite rapidly recovered from the wars. Undoubtedly a great many of the remaining Scots and English settlers were murdered in the rebellion of 1642. Figures, even rough percentages, are of course unobtainable. It would seem probable that the population of Ulster was in the nature of 100,000 in 1642: that perhaps some 10,000 of these were English or Scots living west of the old Scots settlements: and that few of these can have survived the atrocities of the 1640s. Thus the first plantation of Ulster was also, very largely, a failure so far as population was concerned but a success, in the long run, so far as English law and English methods were being gradually accepted as the normal way of conducting legal, economic and to a lesser extent agricultural affairs.

As for the nature, origin and quality of the original colonizers of Ulster in the age of James I and Charles I, there is very little statistical evidence on which to rely. The planted soldiers must have been, in the majority, English or Welsh though they will have included a proportion of Scotsmen: these last must have been mercenaries as opposed to pressed men, since the union of England and Scotland under James I only came into effect with the death of Queen Elizabeth, an event that occurred only a few days before Hugh O'Neill surrendered and which would probably have postponed and perhaps prevented that surrender had he known of the change of dynasty at the time. These soldiers were, in general, the scum of the English and Welsh countryside. Shakespeare knew them well and portrayed them in *Henry the Fifth:* Pistol,

Nym, Bardolph, Fluellen, Macmorris and Boy were good military material but scarcely the types to colonize Ireland or indeed any other portion of the globe though, of course, there were exceptions. In West Cork, many years ago, I met a family with an English name. He was the blacksmith and was proud that an ancestor had been one of the blacksmiths with Mountjoy's army: he still had his forebear's Elizabethan anvil.

As for the servitors, they were Irishmen, either Ulstermen or men from the other three provinces, perhaps younger sons, perhaps themselves uprooted by earlier plantations. Some may have been of Anglo-Norman stock, and thus have inherited a vague knowledge of feudalism, but in language and manners such people had become almost completely Gaelicized by this time. Some may have been of Old English stock: in which case they were Roman Catholics, almost surely, and on their way to becoming as Gaelicized as the Irish descendants of the Anglo-Normans. And some must have been Scots-Irish, from the comparatively prosperous and comparatively peaceful settlements in the eastern and unsequestrated areas of the province. They would be, almost certainly, Presbyterians or even adherents of the more extreme nonconformist faiths such as Anabaptists.

As for the settlers provided by the undertakers, it is equally difficult to define their origins or qualities. From Massachusetts to Botany Bay, the British empire was colonized, at this level, by citizens who were usually regarded as undesirable, as misfits, in their own, increasingly homogeneous, society. Of course there were great English noblemen with Irish estates, from the time of Raleigh to the present day, but since they usually had and have English estates as well they tended and tend to be mere visitors to their Irish lands, the prototype 'absentee landlord'. The men whom the early undertakers found ready to settle the land were of a different type. In the early seventeenth century the undesirable misfit in England was not so much the criminal or prostitute who was later sent to Australia as the man who worshipped God in a manner unacceptable to the authorities. Get them out! Make life uncomfortable for them, so that they go somewhere else! To this must be added the fact that with so many Scots nonconformists already settled in Antrim and Down, with the narrownesss there of the channel and the consequent comparative ease of communication between the settlers and the Lowland Scots, the easiest place for the undertakers to recruit settlers, and thus make money, was undoubtedly Scotland. It is therefore not illogical to assume that the attempt to extend 'loyal' Ulster westwards—as it had been attempted earlier to extend the Pale westwards into King's and Queen's counties—was carried out in large measure by the importation of Scots farmers and their families.

The exception was the County Coleraine. This was, in essence, sold to a consortium of guilds with offices and halls in the city of London, which is why the city and county were renamed Londonderry. Modern comparisons are invariably misleading but, if this is borne in mind, may also be in some measure enlightening. Coleraine was sold to the City much as Katanga in the Congo was 'sold' by the Belgian government to the *Union Miniére*. They could exploit the territory, but must protect it against its own natives, and a share of the profits must revert, positively or negatively by savings in defence, to the metropolitan government. Coleraine was allotted to the City companies on the understanding that this, the heart of the O'Neill country, would be planted and that forts would be built, in particular that Derry—so recently destroyed by Cahir O'Doherty—be turned into an impregnable fortress to safeguard the western part of Ulster. In exchange for great financial privileges, such as Church patronage, the local fisheries and the collection of customs at a nominal cost, the London consortium agreed to police their county and to fortify its towns. As early as 1610 a large body of workmen arrived to rebuild the walls of Derry and to found other fortified centres, significantly named after City companies, such as Draperstown and Salterstown. It may fairly be assumed that the planters they brought in were largely Englishmen. But, to the disappointment of the London government, the businessmen proved as inefficient in the role of military engineers as did the soldiers on the farms. Ten years later the City companies were fined heavily for failing to keep their promises. Londonderry's walls were still unfinished, and no doubt many of their English workmen and farmers were fast sliding into the Irish emotional bog that has embraced so many generations of Englishmen, soldiers and civilians alike.

The problem of what to do with the native Irish in Ulster whose land was escheated was less acute than a similar problem was to prove in parts of that province in the eighteenth century (when great landowners such as Lord Downshire were to 'clear' vast estates of uneconomic peasant-farmers in order to put their farms down for grazing) or in the nineteenth when, again for economic reasons, the eviction of unwanted tenants was almost commonplace all over Ireland and particularly in the west. In seventeenth century Ulster the native population, as already stated, consisted largely of cattle-drovers. Almost all the towns and castles had been burned and very few houses survived the combination of Irish 'scorched earth' policy and the English policy of reprisals. Since the armies of both sides lived off the land, it was the English policy to destroy the crops, the Irish to do likewise when they retreated. Cattle it was possible to hide in the forests, but there can have been few of the beasts left in Ulster in 1608. Sheer starvation drove a part of the population elsewhere in search of food. Some never settled again and it is said to be from these 'broken men' of the sixteenth and seventeenth centuries that many of the tinkers, who still roam the Irish roads and whom foreigners sometimes confuse with Gypsies, are descended. Ulster, after 'the flight of the earls', was in large parts a wilderness, as open to colonization as the lands seized from the Indian tribes in America. Indeed in 1605 Lord Deputy Chichester was thinking principally of Ulster when he remarked that it was foolish for Englishmen to run after empty lands in Virginia, Guiana and elsewhere with Ireland on their doorstep. Sir Arthur, later Baron Chichester, was the prototype of the efficient, honest British colonial governor-general. His family struck root in Ulster during the ten years that he was Lord Deputy. Had Ulster been planted as he wished, that is to say with the minimum of damage to the native Irish population, that first plantation might have endured. But without a civil service to support him and with only a raggle-taggle army that was being rapidly disbanded he had no means to deal with the avarice and incompetence of the undertakers.

Once section of the native population with whom it was more difficult to deal were those freebooters known as swordsmen. These were precisely what their name implies. In pre-English days the value of an Irish chieftain was measured by the number of armed men in his entourage. It was they who raided across the undefined borders and stole their neighbors' cattle or who, when their land was raided, fought the other man's swordsmen. It was they, more or less united for once, who had provided O'Neill with almost all his military strength. And now they still clustered around their old chieftains, impoverished though these were, *bouches inutiles* if the province were to be permanently pacified and a constant menace to settlers and peaceable Irish alike if it were not. They had no role whatsoever to play in Chichester's vision of the new Ulster. Some, it is true, had gone abroad with the earls: others had followed, and it was now that the tradition of the Wild Geese, of Irishmen going to Europe to enlist in foreign armies, began, a tradition which was to drain Ireland of as many, perhaps, as 2,000,000 young men throughout the next two centuries. And this was, from the beginning, actively encouraged by the English authorities. Indeed an attempt was made to export some 6,000 Ulster swordsmen to fight in the Protestant armies of Gustavus Adolphus, but at the last moment the Swedish King shrewdly declined the offer of these reinforcements. It was to the Catholic countries that the Wild Geese usually went, to France above all but also to Spain and Austria, though a few were to be found as far afield as in the Russian service. But meanwhile most of the swordsmen chafed around their petty, impoverished and embittered chieftains in an Ulster that was becoming increasingly an extension of the Scottish lowlands as the settlers moved in.

It was a province rapidly recovering from the ravages of war. The more advanced agronomy of the new colonists enabled more land to be sewn with crops than before: towns were built or rebuilt, the currency was reformed; the exportation of timber began, which was to lead in due course to the destruction of the great forests and thus to yet more land being made available for agriculture; the army, greatly reduced in size, no longer roamed the countryside but was stationed in a series of forts, more properly called blockhouses, which ringed the province, where the soldiers were properly provisioned and even paid, and the religious animosities seemed to be quiescent. It was what is nowadays called a lull. In Ireland such lulls have usually lasted for approximately the life-span of one generation, for the conquered do not forget and though the fathers who fought may be dead or exhausted, the sons also remember: they are taught by their mothers, as they grow up with the ruins of the Castle of Dromore and a score of thousand other ruins before their eyes, that when they are men there will be, for them too, 'work to do'. This lull lasted from 1608 to 1642, the time for a new-born babe to grow to be a man of thirty-four.

Religious animosity during this period of lull was less, probably, than it has been in Ulster at any time since those distant days. The religious division in the Irish wars had first been effectively raised in the South, during the Desmond wars in Munster in the late sixteenth century. But even then the old English of the Pale, though they had generally remained faithful to the Old Faith, had found a more natural affinity for a while with the New English who professed the New Faith. Among the native Irish it was only gradually that the propagandists of the counter-reformation, particularly the English Jesuits, could identify the English enemy with the Protestant enemy. It is said that there is a time-lag in mode of thought between England and Ireland which is dependent on the means of communication but which can nowadays be estimated at quite a short period of time, owing not only a common language but also of course to technological changes. In the sixteenth and seventeenth centuries it took a long time for 'ideas' to reach so remote a province as Ulster, and even longer for the ideologies of the reformation and counter-reformation to be translated into, and understood in, the Irish language. Besides, as pointed out earlier, the Irish at this time were not politically dominated by sectarianism. The country churches were in ruins: the clergy of the Established Church seldom in evidence and unlikely to speak Irish: the Roman Catholic priests, when they were not political agents, generally simple and semi-educated men.

In these circumstances—apart from expelling the Jesuits for purely political reasons—Chichester and his immediate successors saw little point in enforcing the ever harsher religious discriminations that were becoming state policy in England and, to a lesser degree, in Scotland. Presbyterian Ministers were allowed to occupy many of the vacant Establishment Churches, nor did the local bishops, themselves usually Scotsmen and therefore compatriots, often object. The Roman Catholics, the so-called recusants, were also largely left alone, to celebrate the Mass in their own fashion. This tolerance undoubtedly contributed to the duration, and the success, of the lull.

But in England and Scotland tempers were rising on the religious issue, a major contributory factor to the Civil War about to break out in the larger island. In the opinion of this writer while the liberal and Marxist historians' interpretation of the causes behind the English Civil War—the emergence and desire for domination of the *bourgeoisie* —has an element of validity, in Ireland, and indeed in Irish history generally, the economic interpretation has had, and has far less. For the attempts by Chichester's immediate successors, and particularly by Strafford, to enforce the rules of the Anglican establishment through his fiscal policies, both upon the Roman Catholics and upon the non-conformists, not only caused the Catholics to harden in their religion and to identify it with their patriotism but also failed to unite the two subdued religious groups who between them constituted an overwhelming majority in the Province of Ulster.

Indeed in the late 1630s politico-religious issues in England, and above all in Scotland, affected the Scottish settlers to their detriment far more than they did the native Irish. In order to enforce the Church of England ritual upon the Scots, Charles I prepared to invade his second kingdom. In Ireland, his third, this meant a measure of persecution of the Presbyterian and other nonconformist sects which they accepted with great bitterness as they observed the comparative tolerance still extended to the Roman Catholic recusants. By 1641 King Charles had been compelled by *force majeure* (he had no army on which he could rely and could call no parliament which would vote him the money he needed) to give in to the Scots in Scotland. The Scots in Ulster benefited indirectly from King Charles's failure and in one of the many paradoxes of history—the history of Ireland contains more than the histories of most countries—it was the failure of King Charles and his Irish deputies to ram the Church of Ireland down the throats of the Presbyterians and other Ulster nonconformists which led these eventually to turn all their venom against their Roman Catholic neighbors and to become the super-patriots of a Scotland-

England, which they have almost always remained. This 'country' to which they swore and swear allegiance, and for which they were and are prepared to die and even more readily to kill, has never existed. It is the mythical component of an ideology, the reality of which was and is a fear and therefore hatred of the conquered Irish. This has remained an almost constant factor in the Ulster equation. By 1641 it has been estimated that of the three and a half million acres of Ulster, three million belonged, by English law, to Englishmen and Scots. However the proportion of the Ulster population was probably in almost exact reverse. The men who worked the land were dispossessed, Irish-speaking Irishmen. And on their diminished acres the Irish chieftains, with their swordsmen around them, watched the English defeated by the Scots, watched England sliding towards civil war, counted the small numbers of ill-trained soldiers who ringed the province from their blockhouses: communicated with France and Spain: listened to fanatical Counter-reformation priests: and decided that the time had come.

In 1642 Ulster rebelled, under the leadership of Owen Roe O'Neill, the nephew of the greater rebel of that name. Soon enough all Ireland was in flames, and in chaos. And after O'Neill came Cromwell.

The Cromwellian Wars

The second O'Neill rebellion, and the Cromwellian reconquest, were the great traumatic experience in Ulster's, indeed perhaps in all Ireland's, history. This may seem a remote and almost irrelevant chapter of history to English, and even more so to American, readers. But unless the events of 1641 to 1652 are understood, at least at the emotional level, it is impossible to comprehend what lies behind the present and future struggles in what are now the Six Counties of Northern Ireland.

Seldom can there have been a more complex situation, even in Irish history. In Ulster there were at least four politico-religious groups involved: the dispossessed Roman Catholic majority, embittered and since 'the flight of the earls' almost leaderless: the Scots-Irish settlers in the East: the new Scots and English settlers and the 'servitors' in the other counties: and a weak English army, dotted about in its forts and itself rent by the strife in the larger island between Cavaliers and Roundheads.

In Ireland as a whole the situation was equally unamenable to clear-cut division. There, too, at least six forces were involved: the native Irish, partly feudalized long ago but still resentful of English rule: the Anglo-Normans, largely Gaelicized and in large measure indistinguishable from the native Irish: the Old English, particularly of the Pale, almost entirely Roman Catholic and therefore anti-Roundhead though not necessarily pro-Cavalier: the new English of recent plantation, who were not necessarily pro-Cromwellians: a very small English army, also split: and finally the Wild Geese who returned, under Owen Roe O'Neill and others to fight for an Ireland that had, during the lull, almost ceased to exist. A statesman and soldier of genius might have united all these forces. None appeared upon the scene.

Behind all this, but highly relevant, was the Civil War in England, in essence a triangular war between Roundheads, Cavaliers and Scots, fought over issues that did not directly affect the Irish, but which obviously affected them indirectly were they to fail to throw off English rule in the smaller island.

In fact here we have, not for the first time and certainly not for the last, an Irish political situation which was alternately to bewilder, in times of crisis, or to bore, in quieter moments, the English government and people alike. The English had become a very homogeneous people under the Tudor monarchs, the Spanish threat, and the Protestant religion. They had now split on internal, though not on external, issues. From the blood and misery of the Civil War there was, quite quickly, to arise the two-party parliamentary system, which has endured until our time and has been copied in a modified form in England's greatest ex-colony, the United States. Behind this political system there lie certain assumptions, of which two are here relevant. The primary purpose of the two political parties is to decide, by debate and ballot, their relative powers to govern, the principal issues being social and economic—that is to say the redistribution of power or of its easiest symbol, wealth. But when faced by a foreign enemy, whether Spanish, French, German or Russian, the parties tacitly postpone their internal differences until the immediate peril is past.

Therefore, from the English point of view which inevitably they have applied to all their colonies and particularly to Ireland, the art of politics consists in realizing that there are two sides to every question. They are saying so today.

But in colonies, and particularly in Ireland, this assumption is totally untrue. On the one hand there has always been only one side to the question—how to get rid of the conquerors. On the other, in a society fragmented by conquest and colonization, there are numerous sides, almost always in bitter disagreement, as to how this aim should or should not be achieved. It was so in 1641, it is so in Ulster and the Republic of Ireland today.

It is not my intention here to describe the spasmodic, confused and confusing ten-year-war that engulfed almost all Ireland, nor even, in detail, the events in Ulster. Briefly what happened is that in the autumn of 1641 the Roman Catholic population of Ulster rose against the settlers and the military. In the following year, August 1642, Owen Roe O'Neill returned from exile to take command of the Ulster rebel horde, which he transformed into an army of sorts, the only moderately effective army that the Irish possessed. By then much had happened. In that same August civil war had broken out in England, the rebellion in Ireland had spread across the whole island, and a more competent general than Preston, another homing Wild Goose who 'commanded' the Irish army in the south, could quite easily have captured Dublin: a Roman Catholic parliament, the so-called Confederation of Kilkenny, had been assembled in opposition to the Protestant parliament in Dublin: Richelieu's France and other Catholic powers were supplying the Irish with arms and money: and the war in Ireland was becoming ever more a straight religious war, between Catholics and Protestants, almost an extension of the German Thirty Yearsd' War then approaching its climax. Yet to describe events in Ireland during this decade as a war is largely inaccurate, for though there were armies, and even occasional battles and sieges, the Rebellion of 1641 was, like the Rebellion of 1798 and even that of 1919, far closer to a Peasants' Revolt, a *jacquerie*, than to the wars between European sovereign powers in the three centuries to come, with their conventions, even their rules, and their usually clear-cut decision ending in an armistice and ultimately a peace treaty. Indeed it is, perhaps, easier for us to understand the atmosphere of the struggle than it was for our grandfathers: Vietnam is a closer parallel than nineteenth century colonial wars.

It was fought with extreme brutality. Those Protestants who could not flee into Protestant enclaves, such as Dublin, Cork, Bandon and one or two more in the south, to the forts of Ennis-killen or Derry in the north, or to the Protestant settled areas of Antrim and North Down, were usually massacred. This seems to have been particularly so in Ulster, where the Catholics and the Protestants were face to face, where there were few Old English Catholics or Gaelicized Anglo-Normans to act as intermediaries, and where plantation was so recent. It was a war, if war it can be called, fought without gallantry or dignity. And it is hardly surprising that when Cromwell arrived in 1649 he regarded the Irish whom he conquered as little better than dangerous wild beasts, to be exterminated.

It has frequently been said that the most repulsive—emotionally repulsive, that is—aspect of the Nazi genocide of the Jews, Poles and other ethnic groups was its scientific, businesslike efficiency. This is a comprehensible anthropomorphic response. We identify a régime with a human being, and since we tend to regard a man who murders in an outburst of passion or insanity as 'superior' to one who carefully and systematically plans his crime, so we tend to be more horrified by the crimes of the Cromwellians than by those of the Ulster peasantry and swordsmen. This is, of course, totally illogical. The Ulster Old Irish population was as determined upon some form of genocide for the English and Scots in 1641 as were the Ironsides vice-versa ten years later. Indeed the crimes of Cromwell in Ireland have almost certainly been exaggerated in popular mythology: modern historians even deny that he killed the entire population of Drogheda. But Cromwellian atrocities have entered into the people's mind, from which they can now never be erased, while the earlier crimes and massacres by his enemies—which incidentally he invoked specifically as justification for his own—have largely been forgotten, save among the Protestant population of Ulster. And the reason for this brings one back again to the parallel with Nazi Germany.

Cromwell's Ironsides were probably the first army in Europe to be inspired by ideology since the armies of the early Crusades. In Germany, during the Thirty Years' War, appalling atrocities were committed on a far greater scale than in Ireland, but these were savageries of another sort. The principle of *cujus regio, ejus religio* (that it was the religion of the local prince or potentate which counted) did not mean that all his subjects were automatically damned, though they might well be mere objects of loot, rape and murder. It would seem that many, perhaps most, of Cromwell's officers and men regarded the Roman Catholic Irish as damned, as inhuman, as fiends incarnate, an impression strengthened by their knowledge of massacres by these people before their arrival in the strange country. It was therefore their duty to exterminate these monsters in human form, and their utterly wicked religion, just as it was the duty of SS men to exterminate Jews and international Jewry. Like most political slogans, 'Hell or Connaught' meant precisely what it says. If the Roman Catholic population, and particularly the population of Ulster, refused to move out and go to the wilderness of Connaught, then they would be murdered: in which case, in the eyes of the Cromwellian fanatics, they must automatically go to hell, a hell in which those soldiers believed implicitly. Why should they not believe in hell, since they were creating it on the Irish soil? If they preferred to go to Connaught, well then, they could quietly starve to death on their own, out of sight and out of mind. In this writer's opinion, if Cromwell and his people had possessed the technical ability to build gas chambers and drop Zyklon B upon the Irish Roman Catholic subhumans, once they had them at their mercy, they would undoubtedly have used such methods. As it was, they did their best. And this has left a far deeper—as always with the conquerors less than with the conquered, though very deep on both sides—political trauma than had the mere colonization and attempts at rebellion of an earlier and later age. Cromwell and his plantation of Ulster planted more than farmers. It set a time bomb which, re-fused in the nineteenth century, ticks away in that province even today and may, with ill luck or through ill management, have finally blown up before these words are printed.

Only towards the very end of the atrocious war was there any real alliance between the native Irish, particularly the Ulster Irish led by O'Neill, and the Roman Catholic and royalist majority in the south. This alliance, if such it can be called, came too late to affect the political or even the military outcome. It did not come too late to affect the post-war settlement. In the eyes of Cromwell and his successors—he did not linger in Ireland after his initial, successful campaign—they had won a Holy War against the papists, and they set about the creation of a Holy Peace, in an Ireland intended to be without papists. Though they disliked the Church of Ireland and even regarded the Scottish Presbyterians as dangerously High Church, for the Roman Catholics they had little save hatred and contempt. The complete extirpation of the Old Faith in Ireland now became official policy. And since the men who set about enforcing it were neither the miserable military nor the venal businessmen of an earlier age, it seems possible that had they had time they might have succeeded and the Irish might have ceased to exist.

The new policy was threefold. First of all the physical transportation of the Irish to the counties west of the Shannon ('Hell or Connaught') and in particular the expulsion of Roman Catholics from all towns and cities. Secondly a massive and far more effective plantation of the escheated lands east of the Shannon, of which ten counties were allotted to the military, the remainder to the adventurers, while only a handful of 'loyal' Irish were allowed to retain ownership of land, though the dispossessed were in theory to be allotted land in Connaught. This proved to be an administrative impossibility, partly owing to the absence of an effective civil service and even of maps, partly because areas of Connaught were also needed to settle the military colonists. The purpose of this massive transfer of population, similar though of course smaller in scale to that inflicted upon the Germans in Soviet-occupied Eastern Europe after 1945, was to ensure that there were almost no land-owning Roman Catholics east of the Shannon. Total expulsion there proved an impossibility, since with the agricultural technology of the age the new settlers required labor on their farms. But every effort was made to ensure that such Irish as remained would be pauperized, penalized, landless laborers.

Finally a determined attempt was made to stamp out the Roman Catholic religion as such. The few remaining churches were destroyed physically. All priests were now outlawed. Indeed a price of £5 per head of a priest was offered, the same reward as that given for the head of a wolf, for wolves had multiplied in the ruined countryside. Fines for non-attendance at Protestant churches and chapels were enforced. Here again given time the Cromwellians might have been successful, though it seems probable that they came on the scene too late. By 1651 Irish nationalism had become firmly and inextricably intertwined with Roman Catholicism, and the now almost total destruction of the old Gaelic aristocracy and of Gaelic civilization as such meant that the people inevitably looked to their spiritual leaders, the priests, and to the Roman Catholic Church to replace the whole external apparatus of Irish life which was then finally swept away. In no province was his overthrow of old values more violently carried out than in Ulster, where the Protestants were already so deeply entrenched in the east and the Irish so 'wild' in the west: in none did it leave such deep and enduring scars and hatreds.

The Restoration of Charles II in 1660 was greeted by the Roman Catholic majority with joy and the expectation that their wrongs were to be righted, and presumably with a measure of fear on the part of the new Cromwellian settlers. However it was not the policy of the new government, either in England or by extension in Ireland, to put back the clock and restore the *ancien régime*. What restitution of property was made was small and almost exclusively to active royalists in the south, that is to some of the Old English. The Irish received virtually nothing. Although the more virulent attempts to extirpate the Irish ceased, the situation, particularly in Ulster, was more or less frozen so far as the recent plantations were concerned. The new settlers and their Irish serfs lived, uneasily, side by side. And another lull, again to last for some thirty years, ensued.

Religious persecution was relaxed, so far as the Roman Catholics were concerned, but with the passing by the Cavalier Parliament of the so-called Clarendon Code stronger measures were taken to put down the nonconformists. In England it was policy to strengthen the established Church. In Ireland this meant full governmental support for the Church of Ireland. Though this met with a measure of success in the southern provinces, in Ulster the attachment of the two main religious groups to their respective faiths was very great. Thus a triangular situation arose: Church of Rome, Church of Ireland, Nonconformists. That situation has endured to this day. In terms of political logic, the oppressed nonconformists and the oppressed Roman Catholics should have united against their oppressors of the Establishment, just as nowadays in terms of economic logic the oppressed proletariat of both faiths should be united against the boss class. But in the 1670s as in the 1970s such a union of interests by the downtrodden did not take place, for emotional division based on religion and on history was and remains too great. Only very briefly, in the late eighteenth century, inspired by the areligious ideals of the French Revolution and with at least one leader of genius in the person of Wolfe Tone, was it possible for the Irish of all the oppressed faiths to attempt a United Ireland, and even that attempt at national unity was in large measure a failure. But by then much had happened, and much had been repeated. For any student of Irish history the psychological phenomenon called *déja vu* becomes almost a permanent state of mind, and can verge on the obsessive. This can be misleading, for Ulster, though caught in the vice of religious animosity from which it has not yet escaped, was slowly changing, more slowly perhaps than the rest of Ireland and in another direction, far more slowly than England and Western Europe, but changing nonetheless.

During this Caroline lull there was, once again, a rapid and remarkable economic revival in Ulster, more rapid than in the rest of Ireland. When the rating of a country's or a province's economy is zero, as in Ulster in 1651 or in Germany in 1945, a mere return to normality appears to be an economic miracle. This is, however, not the whole story. The Scots settlers and the planted Cromwellians were in general sober, god-fearing, hard-working men. They were good farmers too, and shrewd merchants. It was now that flax became a fruitful crop, and linen a profitable industry. Even today, when one crosses the border, it is striking to see how much better kept the farms in the north are than those to the immediate south. Such is the basic justification of the dour and bigoted Scots-Irish: they are efficient. Cromwellians usually were.

True, the Cromwellian plantation in most of the country and especially in the rural areas soon went the way of the earlier plantations, as the Cromwellian soldiers began immediately to intermarry with Irishwomen. Since in farming communities it is the mother primarily who brings up the children, such marriages bred a new racial mixture, or reinforced the old mixture with new blood, while failing to exterminate old modes of thought and even of behavior. Now began the emergence of that special type of Irishmen called Ulstermen. Their most distinctive quality was and is a siege mentality that has frequently reached paranoiac proportions. Outside of the forts, such as Derry, which were growing into towns, and the almost homogeneous Scots colonies of the east coast, the Ulstermen might be reverting to Irish ways even when retaining the Protestant religion. But the colonists and their descendants were well aware that in Ireland as a whole they were vastly outnumbered and, without British support, were at the mercy of the conquered majority. Since 1641 they also knew how much mercy they might expect. Meanwhile in Ulster, though not in the rest of Ireland, the disfranchised and spoliated Catholics who had not been driven into Connaught were reminded daily that they too were at the mercy of their enemy, and they too knew the nature of that mercy. In this situation qualities and responses came into being which, curiously, united Ulstermen psychologically, if in no other way, and set them apart from most other Irishmen. If a very rough parallel can be drawn, the conquered Irish of Munster, Leinster and Connaught were closer to the Jews of Eastern Europe—diaspora and all—than to the Israelis: the population of Ulster was closer to the present day inhabitants of Palestine, Israeli and Arab alike. Of course, no two situations are ever the same, but the role of America in Israeli affairs is curiously parallel to that of Britain in those of Ulster. It is also to be remarked that in both places this 'siege mentality' produced and produces soldiers and military commanders of the very highest quality.

Thus Ulster began to develop a 'personality' that set it apart not only from Britain, on which its ruling class relied, but also from the rest of Ireland, to which its country folk bore an increasingly closer resemblance. Even Ulster never became a mere extension of England or a Scotland *outre-mer,* while the rest of Ireland quite quickly, and as usual, absorbed most of its foreign conquerors. Nevertheless Cromwell's overthrow of the old order had profound effects which cannot be overestimated in Ireland's history. The determined attempt to expel the Roman Catholics from the towns and cities was only marginally successful: they kept drifting back, and were in any case needed for a mass of menial or semi-menial tasks. On the other hand in the municipalities political power, that is to say the power of the corporations, passed from the hands of the Old English, of the recusants, into those of the new settlers, and was to remain in these hands, in the hands of their descendants, for over two centuries. This has remained the condition in the Six Counties until such time as it shall have been righted by the promised reforms, enforced upon the government of Northern Ireland by the government of the United Kingdom in 1969 and, at the time of writing, being enacted very slowly and amidst growing resentment on the part of Protestant extremists. It is against this rigging of the vote in Derry, Newry, Strabane, Dungannon and of course Belfast itself that the basic campaign of the Civil Rights movement, created in 1968, was first directed. And all this dates from way, way back, from the seventeenth-century concept that in Ireland, and latterly in any part of Ireland controlled by the Crown, it was in the interest of the Crown and, perhaps more important, of basic local political realities that the Roman Catholics be subjected to the Protestants. And it follows from this that trade, and therefore wealth, must be in competent, Protestant hands. The Irish were to be, in their own country, second-class citizens. That they were such inferior persons was already and obviously evident to the English after the Cromwellian plantations, the chance of their remaining so, once 'there was work to do', was a minor consideration, for no pragmatic generation of Teutonic origin thinks beyond its own or its children's lifetime. This Caroline lull lasted for again a generation, and then Ireland blew up once more.

The Stuarts, that most attractive but most inept of British dynasties, had done much harm to Ireland. James I had planted it: Charles I had imposed the tyrannical Strafford upon it: Charles II had failed to redress the wrongs inflicted upon the Irish by his grandfather, his father and the usurper Cromwell: James II, in furtherance of his own aims in the larger island, not only destroyed the new born and very fragile equilibrium that his brother's ministers had helped to create, but also exacerbated religious hatred by his policies, and finally plunged the country into civil war, soon to be followed by international war. He then simply ran away, leaving the Irish to their fate, a nation conquered once again. This deplorable monarch had once been a brave and competent admiral: in Ireland he proved himself a most incompetent and even cowardly soldier. All Ireland had rallied to him save only the key forts of Derry and Enniskillen in Ulster and the Protestant eastern seaboard in that province. (Derry was about to surrender to the Roman Catholic forces in 1689 when the Apprentice Boys seized power within the town, closed the gates, and withstood the siege, an event that is annually commemorated on August 12th of each year.) Any competent general could quite easily have occupied the whole of Ireland, particularly once the efficient and experienced French regiments had arrived to act as a steel backbone for the newly recruited Irish. It was not done. The Ulster coast remained an open beachhead through which King William could pour his English, Scottish, Dutch and other foreign troops, and from which he proceeded to advance southwards and then westwards. He had landed at Carrickfergus with some 36,000 troops on June 14th, 1690. He himself cannot have collected many Ulster volunteers, though some had rallied to his general, Schomberg, who had been in Ulster since the previous winter, for it was only a mere two weeks later that King William's forces met and defeated those of King James at the Battle of Boyne. This was on the 1st of July, new style, but is still celebrated as the great Orangemen's festival on July 12th, the old dating before the Gregorian Calendar reform. It is from this battle, won largely by Danes, Germans and French Huguenots, that the Protestant north derived in large measure its political entity. And it is from the Dutch king, Willem of Orange-Nassau, that the most patriotic and bigoted of Irish Protestants derived their chosen name of Orangemen, their tribal color and, in due course, their semi-secret society known as the Orange Lodges. Though they had not actually fought the battle in any quantities, they had also not surrendered to a Roman Catholic army which however had scarcely bothered to attack them. It is yet another example of the truism that wars are lost, not won. Meanwhile the events, even the dates of these events, have assumed ever since a sacred, indeed an idolatrous, quality in the minds of the Ulster Low Churchman's mythology. This mythology has been used and abused by extremists in Northern Ireland to this day.

ULSTER: IN THE EMPTY HOUSE OF THE STARE[2]

We are closed in, and the key is turned
On our uncertainty; somewhere
A man is killed, or a house burned.
Yet no clear fact to be discerned:
Come build in the empty house of the stare.
WILLIAM BUTLER YEATS

The present media tableau of Ulster has become as fixed and conventional as one of those temperance woodcuts of the last century. Its dramatis personae wring tears from audiences in many countries; but in the United States this flow is a veritable torrent. Americans lament the wretched Catholic minority who are supposed to long, unanimously, for union with "their" country in the South of Ireland; cheers resound from the land of the free for the brave "freedom fighters" (Provisional IRA and Irish National Liberation Army) who—we hear—have unanimous support among the Catholics; hisses are heard for the Protestants because they oppress the Catholics and are nasty, like the Reverend Ian Paisley, and deserve whatever they get from the "freedom fighters"; the loudest boos are saved for the "Brits" who are thwarting a poignant wish to "unify Ireland" while torturing prisoners, shooting innocent civilians, and doing other things too horrible to mention. Among the supernumerary walk-ons are Catholic and Protestant victims and the British soldiers who are murdered in this "fight for freedom"—just the people who "get

[2] Magazine article by Herb Greer, American playwright and author of Irish ancestry. *Commentary.* p 55-64. Ja. '82. Reprinted from *Commentary*, January 1982, by permission; all rights reserved. Copyright by the author.

killed in wars"; the stars are the terrorists, especially those who were starving themselves to death one by one last year. The proper denouement of this melodrama is meant to be an Ireland United and, in the words of the old song, "A Nation Once Again." The awkward fact that such a nation never existed is irrelevant; so is the unpopularity of the "freedom fighters" among Northern *and* Southern Catholics, plus the wish of not a few Catholics to remain citizens of the United Kingdom.

To discover whatever scraps of truth may lie behind this dramaturgy, we must range back into the past. But how far back can we reach for the beginning of the real quandary between these Britannic and Hibernian parts of the British Isles? The very Celts, to whom Irish nationalists look as the true Irish, were first of all "British" invaders, replacing a small dark people known as the Firbolg in the centuries before Christ. But that is perhaps a little too far back. Let us begin rather with the famous "800-year struggle of the Irish nation" which is today touted in the streets of New York and Chicago. This modern legend says that the "freedom fighters" are the heirs of an Irish nation which was invaded by Anglo-Saxon aggressors in the 12th century; it was then ruthlessly oppressed but never extinguished, carrying on through the generations a battle for freedom whose final stage we see now in Ulster's six British counties. For our century, when national-liberation struggles are two-a-penny, mass-produced, and mostly very recent, this must be the hoary grand old man of them all.

To speak of the 12th-century Irish nation is something like speaking of the 20th-century Arab nation. The traditional "kingdoms" of Ireland resembled nothing that we know by that name. Individually and severally they were a crazy quilt of phratric territories and influences, without a political center of gravity and devoid of any popular sense of national unity or identity. The tribes did share a common Celtic language and a certain cultural style and pattern of customs. Their Christian religion, however, was a European import, brought in earlier by a British monk who is now called St. Patrick, and heavily diluted with local paganism. The society was savage and extremely primitive by contemporary European standards; the title of High King carried no administrative or even nominal authority over the whole island, where loyalties were purely personal and tribal.

The "Saxon invaders" of nationalist legend were neither Saxon nor invaders. They were the Norman French who, under William the Conqueror, had destroyed the Anglo-Saxon kingdom in the 11th century. William's descendant, Henry II of England, when authorized by Pope Adrian IV to "enter Ireland," did not do so. At the invitation of an Irish chieftain, Dermot MacMurrough of Leinster, a thousand Normans under Richard Fitzgilbert, Earl of Clare (called Strongbow), crossed the Irish Sea in 1170, to help MacMurrough in a local dispute. Strongbow married MacMurrough's daughter and succeeded to his rule in Leinster. Only then did Henry II travel to Ireland, to confirm the royal authority over his vassal Fitzgilbert. This led to the extension—by treaty—of the English king's suzerainty into Ireland. The Gaelic chieftains did not rise up against this but agreed to it willingly. The arrangement was endorsed by Pope Alexander III in 1172, and three years later Rory O'Connor, the High King, put his name to it.

English administration of Ireland, such as it was, centered on the old Viking city of Dublin, and did not run far. The Norman baronies accepted only a nominal overlordship of the English king, and beyond them the tribal territories were left to themselves. In time the Norman settlers took up the local language and customs, and were absorbed into the tribal system, to become themselves Irish. We have had a souvenir of this process in the Norman French middle name of John Fitzgerald Kennedy.

I do not propose to drag the reader through the whole complex history of the British "presence" in Ireland, stage by bloody stage. But it should be remembered that when rebellions occurred, particularly in the early days, they were more often mounted by English settlers and their descendants than by Gaels, and were fought on the assumption that military force was a legitimate means of establishing sovereignty—for the crown as well as for the rebels. These uprisings (which were by no means continuous) were not rooted in any nationalist cause. In principle the Irish had no objection to the titular authority of a foreign king. The "Crown of Ireland" was offered at various times to Norway, Scotland, France, and even Austria. Fighting in Ireland was liable to break out in disputes over land, over the rapacity of crown administrators, or—where English power was weak or indifferent—a tribal chieftain might try to reassert and broaden his influence. This was the case with the great rising of the Ulster "king," Hugh O'Neil, against Elizabeth I at the end of the 16th century. But he was defeated as the 17th century dawned, and the tribal system was broken forever. In all these conflicts the common people suffered horribly, cursing the rebels as often as they damned the English. There was no more national solidarity at the grass roots than at the top—where there was none at all.

After the Reformation, the Catholic powers of Europe attempted to use Ireland as a back door into Protestant Britain. This threat to the security of the crown sparked a more positive English involvement in Ireland and was an important reason for the "planting" of English settlers on Irish soil. The most successful of these ventures were the 1609 Plantation of Ulster and the 17th-century settlements in Ireland after the Cromwellian civil war.

Some writers have given the impression that these plantations involved a mass displacement of the local Irish by a solid phalanx of English and Scots invaders. What actually happened was rather a filtering in of newcomers among the native Irish, who were constantly present and used as labor on the land which had been confiscated for the settlers. This mingling did not lessen hostility between Catholic Irish and Protestant settlers, but inflamed it, especially in Ulster where many settlers were as plebeian as the locals. Feeling cut off from their mother country amid a dangerous alien population, these Northern Protestants developed that mixture of sectarian hatred and stubborn self-reliance which still survives today. But the sectarian conflicts of the 17th century were not a matter of Irish nationalism. In the civil wars of that period Irish Catholics fought alongside English Papists, not for an independent Ireland but for the Stuart kings of England. They lost, first to Cromwell and then to William of Orange (who was not English), and suffered the fate of the losing side: penal laws barred them from politics and the ownership of land.

It is one of the many ironies of Irish history that when a real nationalist movement did appear at the end of the 18th century, it came out of the Protestant community, partly as a protest against the English parliament's suppression of trade and business in Ireland. Wolfe Tone and his fellow rebels tried to make an Irish revolution on the French model, with the help of an anti-clerical French government and in the face of bitter condemnation from the Catholic clergy. The enterprise was a somewhat intellectual, middle-class effort with no popular base; it quickly degenerated into sectarian butchery and resulted in the formal Union of Great Britain and Ireland in 1800. A popular sense of Irish nationalism did begin to emerge after that, most prominently under the leadership of Daniel O'Connell; but this was part of a general birth of such feelings among European peoples, and did not express itself in any popular wish to separate Ireland from the British imperial crown. This was so inside Ireland even after the great mid-19th-century famine.

It was the huge Malthusian nightmare of the famine, more than anything else, which contributed to the image of a cynical Britain turning its back on the suffering Irish and so fostering Irish nationalism. In fact the system of loose rule through local oligarchies had always been common to the whole of the United Kingdom. The width of the Irish Sea made it looser in Ireland than in mainland Britain; this was the main cause of the long history of maladministration and official corruption on the island—though it should be said that the opportunities for corruption and chicanery were taken up as eagerly by the Irish as by British officials. It has been suggested that the British government deliberately engineered the starvation of about a quarter of the Irish population in the middle of the 19th century and forced another quarter to emigrate. This is the general view of American descendants of the emigrants, providing most of the emotional fuel for American support of violent Republican groups. Like many an atrocity story in nationalist mythology, this charge of genocide has a *prima facie* plausibility; but it will not stand serious examination.

It is true that the British authorities were not deeply troubled by the agonies of the Irish poor. They were, however, equally indifferent to their own lower classes. The first great public-health campaign in the United Kingdom, after the 19th-century cholera epidemics, succeeded not through official compassion but because foul living conditions and disease threatened to wipe out an important section of the labor force. No such consideration applied in Ireland. Out of sight across the Irish Sea, the poor there were tenant farmers at the bottom of a many-layered system of land tenure, with an agricultural economy that was too inflexible to support the population—depending as it did on the single food crop of potatoes. When this failed the whole structure collapsed, and the British government was simply unable to grasp the nature and scope of the disaster. It seemed at first just another of the periodic sharp famines which the Irish had suffered before and survived. When some inkling of its extremity did seep through, there was no practical sense of how to help on the necessary scale, or even that such help was possible. It would have required a vast aid operation of late 20th-century proportions—something unimaginable at the time, without a ready and deep-seated belief that these large numbers of poor, useless as a labor force, were worth a gigantic effort and expense, just because they were human beings.

For us to whom compassion has become a basic political principle, that is taken for granted. It was not so in the mid-19th century. This may make it easier to understand why attempts to help the Irish (there were some) proved limited and not very effective; and why rent, in the form of edible produce, was being shipped out of Ireland at the very height of the famine. To portray the calamity as cold-blooded murder is exciting melodrama but bad history.

Of course the victims were not looking at history. They were trapped as participants in a grim spectacle of families reduced to mutual cannibalism; roads littered with the skeletal bodies of those who had died with their mouths full of grass; forced evictions which meant joining those corpses on the highway; desperate famished mobs outside the workhouse, waiting for death inside to give them a place and some faint hope of life; and luckier survivors, uprooted from their land, sailing under often appalling conditions to find better hopes in the New World. The collective memory of these ordeals and other horrors, was carried by emigrants to America and carefully preserved in their folk traditions, along with an utterly implacable hatred of the British whom they blamed for it all. It is no wonder that their descendants see the British as cartoon monsters, pitiless "Saxon" tyrants to be hunted out of Ireland like wild beasts.

Ulster has from the earliest times been a peculiar place. It seems to have offered the stiffest resistance to Celtic invasion, and its later trade and cultural relations were sometimes closer with the Western isles of Scotland than with the rest of Ireland. The topography of Ulster protected it from Norman domination, and it put up the last effective resistance to the English in the time of Elizabeth I. Her garrison line against Hugh O'Neill ran from Newry to Lough Erne, not very far from the present border.

The 17th-century settlements of English and Scots on the island made Ulster exceptional in other ways. Most of Ireland was grounded on a Gaelic-speaking peasantry ruled by Protestant landowners who spoke English. (This was also the language of the small middle class, Catholic and Protestant alike.) Only in the northeast did Protestantism have a secure popular base. The traditional hostility between Papists and Protestants was sealed with agrarian violence between night-riding societies like the Peep O'Day Boys (later to become the Orange Order) and the Catholic Defenders. A sort of white-trash mentality grew up among poorer Ulster Protestants: no matter how low they sank, they could still look down on the Taigs, or Catholic peasants.

Ulster was the only province of Ireland to benefit from the industrial revolution, with a flourishing linen manufacture and a powerful shipbuilding industry. These softened the impact of the 19th-century famine in the North and, with the increasing solidarity of the Protestant community, strengthened Ulster's popular links with the United Kingdom.

Sectarian hatred was not eased by 19th-century administrative reforms which restored Catholic access to politics and land. Most Protestants were further unsettled by the emergence of a Home Rule movement (Home Rule meant an Irish parliament with certain local powers of legislation and administration, under the suzerainty of Britain's crown and parliament. Something like this had existed as early as the 16th century, but now Protestants feared a huge and enfranchised Catholic majority on the island.) and, after the famine, by extremist groups like Sinn Fein and the Irish Republican Brotherhood who were determined to create an independent Ireland by armed force. Drawing most of their support from America, these wilder activists took up the tactics of assassination and terrorism being used by other such conspiracies in Europe. Their Jacobin approach was furiously castigated by the Catholic Church.

The amazing obtuseness of the British government over Home Rule (an arrangement which was not, after all, unprecedented in Ireland) gave Republican extremists time to consolidate. It also allowed the Ulster Protestants enough time to set up a formidable resistance to Home Rule, with an armed militia and a well-orchestrated political campaign to keep Ireland in the United Kingdom. Even the relatively mild Home Rule Bill of 1921 (it was the third try in twenty-six years; the others had been killed by opposition in Britain and from Irish Protestants) was rejected by the Ulster Protestants as "disastrous to the well-being of Ulster . . ., subversive of our civil and religious freedom, destructive of our citizenship, and perilous to the unity of the Empire."

Sir Edward Carson, who led the movement against Home Rule, was not a bawling redneck figure like the Reverend Ian Paisley. He was a solidly respectable Dublin lawyer with wide public support not only among Irish Protestants but over the whole of Great Britain. He was backed by the opposition Conservative party under Bonar Law, by key figures in the Liberal government first under Asquith and then under Lloyd George, and by important areas of the civil service and units of the British army, which would have to enforce any Home Rule Bill against the Protestant militia. During the so-called Curragh Mutiny of 1914 it became clear that a significant part of the British army in Ireland was not prepared to do this, and the issue brought the United Kingdom to the very edge of civil war. This awful possibility was averted by war with Germany and a parliamentary stay on Home Rule until that conflict was over.

Naturally the Catholic population of Ireland, and some middle-class Protestants, were in favor of Home Rule. But this still did not imply a separation from the British crown. The activists who favored a Republic were an unpopular tiny minority, opposed by the Catholic Church and rather unsavory even by our own criteria of national-liberation movements. The proto-fascist mouthings of Patrick Pearse about blood and soil evoke a familiar sort of nausea when one reads them today.

Much has been made of the British government's stupidity in killing Pearse and some of the other rebels after the 1916 Republican insurrection in Dublin. These executions were not extraordinary in a year when the British army suffered 60,000 casualties in a few hours—among whom were Irish Catholics and Protestants of the Ulster Division—in a famous battle against German forces on the Somme. Roger Casement was known to have tried to form a kind of Waffen-SS with Irish prisoners of war, and the Germans were openly hailed as "glorious allies" by the 1916 rebels. The British parliament's fatuous move of passing a bill for Irish conscription during the war, plus the sympathy stirred by the executions—Yeats's "a terrible beauty is born, " and so on—no doubt helped the politics of independence. But so did Allied propaganda about World War I as a crusade for the self-determination and liberty of small peoples, and the general mood which this aroused after the war, both in Ireland and in the rest of the United Kingdom.

The IRA campaign from 1919 to 1921 against British administration of Ireland was unique on two counts. It was the first large-scale, sustained, and successful terrorist operation of modern times. It was also the first such clash in which news media played a more important part than military strength. There could be no question of the ill-disciplined and somewhat ragtag IRA matching either the Royal Irish Constabulary or the British army in open warfare; so a deliberately cruel and gruesome series of assassinations, atrocities, and small-scale harassments was mounted, together with a social boycott of the police enforced by ferocious intimidation. The object was to break the discipline of the crown forces (most of whom were Irish, largely Catholic) and provoke reprisals which would anger the population.

It took about six months to break police morale in the South. The reaction was then vicious and wholesale, and came not only from the police and their notorious auxiliaries, the Black and Tans, but from the British army. What were probably the worst of these incidents, many of which made sensational headlines in Britain and Ireland, happened in 1920. Villagers in the countryside, fearing reprisals during the night, went out to sleep in haystacks and hedges. Late in the year, following an IRA massacre

in Dublin of twelve British officers, two auxiliaries, and one innocent veterinary officer, the crowd at a Dublin Gaelic football
match in Croke Park was surrounded by the Royal Irish Constabulary and some auxiliaries. The officers were supposed to search
for IRA gunmen. Instead they fired into the crowd, killing twelve
civilians. The same night two IRA prisoners were killed by the
police at Dublin Castle, along with a civilian who had been picked
up at a nationalist haunt in the city. In December crown forces,
taking revenge for a terrorist outrage, burned out and destroyed
the whole center of Cork.

In Ulster, Protestant mobs attacked Catholic ghettos with
bloody results. Being more defensive in the North, the nationalist
campaign was consequently less effective; but the general strategy
of the IRA was brilliantly successful. The Irish public was infuri-
ated, and the British across the water, reading lurid accounts of
what their own people were doing, expressed pained indignation,
directed in great part at the British government and forces. As
now, when cold-blooded atrocity and hot-blooded retaliation were
weighed in a moral and political balance, the greater weight of ob-
loquy pulled down the reprisal. This repercussion was compound-
ed by the celebrated hunger strike of Cork's Lord Mayor, Terence
MacSwiney. Arrested at an IRA conference, he protested at military interference with an elected civil official (though MacSwiney
was in fact the local commanding officer of the IRA), and tem-
pered the protest with a fast of seventy-three days. There were
other hunger strikers, some of whom also died, but MacSwiney's
lingering death—seen as an impressive example of moral courage
and the stubbornness of Irish national feeling—most profoundly
affected British and Irish popular opinion.

The Catholic Church, typically, reacted to the troubles with
political circumspection. Condemning a terrorist murder in 1919,
the Archbishop of Cachel remarked that even if the British had
been committing outrages in Ireland, two wrongs did not make a
right. What the IRA were counting on, of course, was for two
wrongs to make a Republic. This species of political judo is a matter of habit these days, but it was novel then.

The extremists did not get their Republic. Southern Ireland,
with its massively nationalist Catholic population, was too much

trouble for Britain to keep; Ulster in the North, with its fierce, well-armed and organized Protestants (who still commanded immense popular support in Britain), was too much trouble to let go. Because Ireland had for centuries been vital to the security of Britain and still was, the 1921 treaty which set up the Irish Free State kept certain ties with Britain; a common citizenship was retained, as was a parliamentary oath of loyalty to the crown, and Britain was given port facilities on Ireland's Atlantic coast. Six of Ulster's nine counties were excluded from Free State jurisdiction and given a peculiar Home Rule. Besides sending regular MP's to represent its electorate in London, the province had its own parliament at Stormont, subject to the authority of Westminster—an authority which in practice was seldom exercised.

There was provision for union of the six counties with the rest of Ireland if Stormont should agree, but this clause was disingenuous under the circumstances. Since the 17th century, Protestants had been privileged above all in Ulster, and the Catholics had not taken it passively. In rural terrorism and then in urban riots, plenty of blood had been shed over the years, on both sides of the religious abyss. With revenge and counter-revenge become a tradition, it is easy to imagine how Protestants saw their fate under a government overwhelmingly dominated by their old sectarian enemies. After the signing of the Free State Treaty they watched a violently dissenting minority in the South—the anti-treaty Republicans—being mercilessly cut to pieces.

The Irish civil war of 1922-23 was bloodier and uglier than the fight against the British, with savage atrocities on both sides. For example, the Free State government sanctioned the summary killing of Republican prisoners. If the Catholics could treat their own like that, what would they do to those who had been their oppressors for centuries? This fear certainly contained an element of bad conscience, and was all the worse for that.

There was some effort in the North toward calming the old enmities. James Craig, the first Prime Minister at Stormont, made a number of conciliatory declarations. Lord Carson himself had said: "From the outset let us see that the Catholic minority have nothing to fear from the Protestant majority. . . .While maintaining intact our religion, let us give the same rights to the religion of our neighbors." These sentiments remained, as one might say, inoperative. First of all, the Catholic nationalists in the North—about a third of the population—refused to recognize or take part in the new administrative system, or vote in its elections. Then came Eamon De Valera's Irish Constitution in the South, claiming sovereignty over the six counties, and containing the ominous Article 44:

The state recognizes the special position of the Holy Apostolic and Roman Church as the guardian of the faith professed by the great majority of the citizens. . . .

This was no dead letter. The Catholic hierarchy was able to meddle with effect in the political life of the South, suppressing legislation which it found objectionable, imposing censorship on literature and the arts, while preventing divorce or the sale or distribution of any form of birth-control device. These and other symptoms of social and political influence helped the Northern Protestants to feel justified in their own ruthless oppression of the Catholic minority, and to accept more cheerfully its self-imposed exclusion from the political life of the province.

The intractability of the situation was acknowledged by Republicans even before the Free State Treaty was ratified. In August 1921, De Valera himself had told his colleagues that some of them had neither the power nor the inclination to use force with Ulster. It would, he said, be making the same mistake that the British had made in Ireland. This was a rare injection of reality into Republican discourse, but it was matched by a political *mesquinerie* which grew more intense as time wore on, widening the rift between Ulster and the South. After Britain gave up its Irish port facilities in 1938, De Valera kept his government officially neutral in the war against the Axis powers. There were accusations that he allowed the Germans to use the Irish coast as a haven for submarine action against Allied shipping, but these were never proved. Certainly he did permit the German representative in Dublin to send weather reports to the Luftwaffe, and these helped in the bombing of Britain and Ulster. Like Joseph Kennedy, the American Ambassador to Britain, De Valera did what he could to keep the United States out of the war. When his efforts failed, he protested at the presence of American troops in Ulster as an "infringement of Irish sovereignty." No such protest was made after the heavy German air attacks on Belfast.

As late as 1944, the American State Department said bluntly: "Despite the declared desire of the Irish government that its neutrality should not operate in favor of either of the belligerents, it has in fact operated and continues to operate in favor of the Axis powers." Upon learning of the death of Hitler, De Valera called on the Nazi minister in Dublin to express sympathy, insisting loftily that this was a neutral act of protocol. As the *New York Times* put it: "Considering the character of the man for whom he was expressing grief [and considering that 50,000 Southern Irishmen had volunteered for service in the British forces] . . .there [was] obviously something wrong with the protocol, the neutrality, or Mr. DeValera." For Ulstermen, many of whom died in the war against Hitler, and more of whom suffered under German bombs at home, these antics did nothing to bring Ulster and the Republic closer together as a "free nation."

The IRA had stayed unofficially alive after the Irish civil war of 1922-23, involving itself in desultory terrorism both in Ireland and—once World War II had started—in Britain. It became a pro-Axis underground organization, dedicated mainly to the support of Germany, while its titular "Chief of staff" traveled to the Third Reich for instruction in the art of making bombs. The IRA reached out to Hitler as Wolfe Tone had once reached out to Napoleon, but Hitler's spies in Ireland had a low opinion of their would-be comrades-in-arms. The most important of these German agents, Herman Goertz, said: "In spite of the fine qualities of individual IRA men, as a body I consider them worthless." Their clumsiness and indiscretion caused De Valera to intern 400 of their number, probably in the fear that their activity would provoke Allied intervention in Southern Ireland. But the IRA survived that, remaining true to the old Irish tradition of secret societies.

For several years after the war the one-party state of Northern Ireland enjoyed relative calm. This was guaranteed in part by the 1922 Special Powers Act, a bit of police-state legislation passed to cope with terrorist attacks and never taken off the books. It was enforced by the Royal Uster Constabulary, a predominantly Protestant force with an armed auxiliary called the B Specials who must have been—from the Catholic point of view—something like a gang of peckerwood deputy sheriffs let loose among Southern American blacks. The postwar supremacy of the Protestants was entrenched by measures like the Elections and Franchise Act of 1947, which among other things made it possible for one elector to have six local government votes, and by a system of gerrymandering which insured Protestant majorities on the councils of cities where Catholics outnumbered Protestants.

From 1955 to 1962 there was an upsurge of IRA activity against the six counties, the so-called Border Campaign. It sent the North into a state of armed alert and angered the government of the Republic. (Under De Valera the Irish Free State gradually dropped most of its connections with Britain, so transforming itself into the Republic, and never giving up its claim to the North.) After a spate of minor incidents at customs posts and other installations, and the blowing up of a BBC transmitter, the campaign fizzled out. There was no popular support for violent "unification" in Ulster, where the British welfare state had given Catholics a far higher standard of living than their follows in the underdeveloped South. IRA men were interned at the Curragh camp in the Republic, and their organization once more subsided into its underground mode, dedicated in the North to protecting Catholics during sectarian riots. The next fit of terrorism in the North was to unfold in quite a different way.

Since de Tocqueville it has become common place that political protest and insurrection are not ignited by the despair of the oppressed, but by the prospect of an end to that despair. The year 1968 was brimming with such prospects, most of which were to be cruelly perverted. Those which surfaced in Northern Ireland were no exception.

On both sides of the border there had been efforts to break out of old attitudes. Irish President Sean Lemass and Northern Prime Minister Terence O'Neill exchanged visits in 1965, groping toward a friendlier relationship rather than instant unification. Ulster's Nationalist party responded by accepting the role of official opposition at Stormont; but Protestant Unionists, whom O'Neill had not consulted, boiled over. An extremist faction began to dispute O'Neill's leadership and a Protestant equivalent of the IRA appeared, calling itself the Ulster Volunteer Force. Proscribed under the Special Powers Act, it carried on like the IRA, as a secret society. In 1966 a demagogue and hellfire preacher, the Reverend Ian Paisley, stood up to contest the leadership of the *verkrampfte* Protestants. Like the rest of Britain, Northern Ireland was affected by a general sagging of morale in the 60s. In Carson's time the tightest bond between the province and the rest of the United Kingdom had been a common imperial citizenship. Now the empire was gone, and Britain was under economic and political strain, with its social fabric showing signs of wear. This pervasive mood of uncertainty, and the uncharacteristic quarrels among the Protestant majority, formed the background to a late-60s ferment which the students of Ulster shared with those elsewhere.

It was a measure of how things were changing that the protesting students did not organize against the partition of Ireland as such. Inspired by the Paris fulminations of May 1968, they joined a civil-rights movement founded two years before on the American model, with the Catholic minority as cognate to American blacks. The outstanding bones of contention were symptoms of Catholic second-class citizenship: discrimination in jobs and housing, the political chicanery which denied proper representation to Catholics, and so on. The protest in effect endorsed partition with a demand that Catholics should have the same political and social rights as other Britons. But it was partition which had nailed down Protestant denial—and Catholic rejection—of those rights in the first place, so the two issues could not be so neatly separated. From the beginning there was a Republican element in the movement.

O'Neill responded to the protest and tried to liberalize Northern Ireland with anti-discrimination reforms. In retrospect, the assumption that with a few administrative measures it was possible to sweep away a long tradition of injustice, social abuse, and malice seems absurd. But the expectation was encouraged by the media above all. Nevertheless the reforms were stalled by popular opposition before O'Neill himself was deposed as Unionist leader, and then they were outpaced by another sort of action. The civil-

rights people had their own extremists, who in October 1968 ma-
nipulated the movement into an illegal march from Belfast to Londonderry. They did this with the expectation that it would
provoke violent Protestant reaction and draw the attention of the
media. It was the old IRA tactic of 1919, in a more passive and
devious mode. The gambit paid off handsomely, with bloody rioting at Burntollet Bridge and then in Londonderry and Belfast, in
which undisciplined police became involved on the side of Protestant goon squads and mobs. This eventually forced the intervention of the British army. It also gave birth to the Provisional IRA,
when the "Official" IRA failed to protect Catholics during the
fighting and then opted for an unusually constitutional approach
to the problem of partition. Feeding on blind hatred, terrorist violence grew among Catholics and Protestants. When the Stormont
regime proved finally unable to cope with these atavistic spasms,
it was dissolved, bringing the province under the direct rule of
Westminster.

Spectacular coverage of the urban *jacquerie* first sketched and
set the outlines of the tableau with which I began this essay. The
main beneficiaries of the media dramaturgy (which closely paral-
lels terrorist propaganda) are the Provisional IRA and the self-
styled "Marxist" Irish National Liberation Army which appeared
in the 70s. (The Provos and the INLA are "armies" in the same
sense that the Symbionese Liberation Army was a military force.
Actually they are murderous secret societies in the classic Irish
mold.) Their goal had been consistent throughout the last decade
and is the same today. It is to exasperate and discourage British
public opinion, while fomenting pressure outside the United
Kingdom (mainly in America) for Britain to "do something," i.e.,
turn the six counties over to the Republic. The political credit for
this is then to be used to manage a gradual takeover of Ireland,
after which its rather too British manner of government can be
transmogrified into something more in accord with the fancy of
the terrorists. As Mussolini said of himself and Italy in 1932: their
aim is simple; they wish to govern Ireland and their stoutest backing in this noble enterprise comes not from Ireland but from the
United States. It ranges from Tip O'Neill and some of his more
moderate colleagues to the Irish National Caucus (led by that

great Irish-American Mario Biaggi) and Noraid, whose propaganda calls up memories of Fritz Kuhn and his 1930s German-American Bund, who supported Hitler with money and heart-wrenching atrocity stories about the 'oppressed' German minority in the Sudetenland. Alone among fascist cabals in Europe who are actually killing people, the Provos and the INLA depend upon the generous financial and moral support of Americans.

The activities which the worst of the American cheerleaders are happy to excuse include wholesale destruction of property by arson and explosives; kidnapping; sectarian murder; ambushing and individual assassination of police officers, troops, political figures, and diplomats and the random slaughter of civilians with bombs. Much of the media coverage in Britain and America has also given Irish terrorism a certain aura of legitimacy, most offensively through television interviews in which criminals are given approximately the same treatment as some leaders of the opposition; by comments like that of *Newsweek's* Tony Clifton, who demanded on television that the British "get out of Ireland"; and in the gullible treatment of stage-managed incidents in Ulster, which depend upon what a bemused (London) *Sunday Times* journalist of Irish extraction called "the instant and expert mendacity to which journalists and no doubt other interested parties . . .are treated in episodes of this sort." An egregious case in point was Bloody Sunday in 1972, falsely projected as a gratuitous attack by British troops on unarmed and peaceful civilians. This lie is still believed in the United States and by a surprising number of people in Britain. (The IRA maneuvered civilians in between themselves and troops, then opened fire. Seven civilians and six IRA men were killed by return fire. Surviving terrorists removed the weapons of the dead IRA men and withdrew, leaving apparently innocent "civilian" bodies.)

Some sections of the media have enhanced the image of the terrorists by treating them as a "side" equivalent to the British government, carrying as it were an equal weight of sovereignty. *Newsweek* is one of the most careless in this respect, and has done other odd things. When the magazine published a moving photograph of a masked Catholic child waving his fists in front of a wall of flame, I wrote to its British headquarters, pointing out that the

London *Observer* had photographed newsmen apparently in the act of staging that picture, using a pile of burning barrows in a vacant lot. *Newsweek* offered in reply their photographer's story that he had, in the company of all those newsmen (they included TV men carrying sound equipment at the ready), just happened to "come upon" the spectacle. This is rather like the insistence of ABC-TV that it interviewed a hunger striker's daughter in preference to other Ulster children because she just happened to be "articulate." At least one New York newspaper has published bald fiction about the British army in Ulster disguised as news. The Boston *Globe,* caught out publishing a lie in its report of the attack on Bernadette Devlin MacAliskey, was so embarrassed that it rethought its editorial approach to Ulster. A BBC TV magazine program, *Panorama,* broadcast in September what amounted to a party political show for the Provisional IRA—just at the point when the "anti-H-Block" hunger strike was collapsing and the terrorists badly needed such a public-relations coup. In this program blame for stubbornness during the hunger strike was attached to the British government. Even the *Times* of London once went so far as to report two murders and an attempted murder in Ulster as a military "offensive." A certain amount of reportage for other countries has more to do with an itch to get in on some hot action—reporters create the action if necessary, with bribes—than with any concern for truth or victims or anything else in Ulster.

Despite this plethora of complaisant and occasionally corrupt journalism, the terrorists have signally failed to repeat the success of 1919-20. Initially sectarian killings were matched in kind by Protestant terrorists, as were bomb attacks. But such reprisals are no longer mounted on the same scale. The demoralized Royal Ulster Constabulary gave up its duties to the army while the B Specials were disbanded and the main force reorganized. It has now returned to its normal duty of policing the community. In defiance of extraordinary provocation, notably the Warren Point massacre (in which eighteen soldiers were murdered with radio-controlled bombs) and the killing of Lord Mountbatten with some of his family, army discipline has on the whole remained tight and professional throughout these troubles. Where soldiers have been caught in violation of standing orders or committing crimes, they have been arrested and tried.

Without the cachet of constant brutal reprisals, terrorist violence has proved counterproductive even in the Catholic community. The "hard men" are regarded as heroes by their friends and by some of the more obstinate Republicans. But the community at large, North and South, recognizes these people as remorseless butchers of human beings. Finally, as the whole world knows, they resorted to a desperate tactic in order to change this image. While the sniping, bombing, and murder continued, a formidable public-relations exercise was constructed around convicted terrorists in the Maze prison who engaged in a campaign of hunger strikes, aiming to recapture the moral appeal of Terence Mac-Swiney and cash in on the natural compassion inspired by the spectacle of men dying in public. The ploy drew enormous publicity abroad, sympathy in Britain and the Republic, and frenzied support among the American Irish. All this climaxed when one of the hunger strikers managed to win an Ulster by-election before committing suicide. As the cynical nature of the operation became clearer, the original sympathy was infused with a kind of embarrassed discomfiture, though Northern Ireland remains more than ever polarized along sectarian lines. Even though demonstrations concurrent with the deaths shrank in size, Bobby Sands's preterrorist election agent did succeed in winning the Fermanagh and South Tyrone seat vacated by Sands's death—after the principal Catholic party had been shunted out of the election.

The suicidal terrorists have reaped praise from many quarters, some predictable, others surprising, on the grounds that their "sincerity" is somehow worthy of "respect" and makes them "right" in some way. Before the hunger strikes it was the violence which proved the sincerity and the sincerity which justified the violence. Once the "brave boys" who were in prison for slaughtering other people and shooting soldiers in the back started killing themselves as well, it was their willingness to die—on the orders of their organization—which drew admiration, which in turn rubbed off on their "cause." There have been other such "sincere" martyrs in modern times. Horst Wessel was one, and a closer parallel could be found in the deaths of Andreas Baader and Ulrike

Meinhof. Their suicides too were followed by claims that they had been "murdered" by the authorities.

The Catholic hierarchy, after an ambiguous spell of objecting to violence in general—including the defensive violence of the British forces—while supporting the "nationalist" aims of the terrorists, at last found the hunger strikes too much to take. Following several deaths of hunger strikers and consequent civilian casualties, Cardinal O'Fiaich and his bishops denounced the campaign outright, being careful as always to assail the British government in their terms of reproof. In the lower echelons of the priesthood it is still possible to find a casuistic defense of the suicides on the ground that they were not really "intended"; the "intention" was political status, or British compliance with "five just demands" which amount to the same thing. In the longer term there is of course the "intention" to unify Ireland, change its government, and so on.

After the hunger strike collapsed early in October, the terrorists reverted to type with a bombing campaign in London; they murdered one old woman and an Irish Catholic teenager, while maiming a number of soldiers and the Commandant General of the Royal Marines. The same IRA 'active service unit' then planted a booby-trapped toy in the street near a London school. This exploded in the hands of a woman who happened to pick it up. In mid-November they killed Reverend Robert Bradford, a British MP from Belfast. In July of this year, angered by the British victory in the Falkland Islands (pro-Argentine graffiti had appeared in Republican areas of Belfast), the Provos detonated two more bombs in central London, killing a number of soldiers on ceremonial duty and horribly maiming civilian bystanders. These activities of 'The Bold Fenian Men' are supposed to contribute to a long-term objective of unifying Ireland and installing their own fascist brand of government on the island.

Unification is in any event a false issue now, since the Irish government has no desire to haul Ulster, with its vast expenses and its large body of violent and terrified Protestants, into the Republic. No doubt the cry, "Ireland is One," will continue to be heard, if the present Finn Gael majority in the Irish Dail (parliament) collapses and a Fianna Fail administration is returned to office. (Finn Gael and Fianna Fail are the two principal political parties in the Republic. Finn Gael is descended from the protreaty party which formed the Irish Free State. Fianna Fail is the offspring of the anti-treaty forces who lost the civil war, and claims to be more "Republican.") But the cry cannot, as we have seen, denote the restoration of amounts to a demand for geographical symmetry, so that the shores of the Hibernian Island match the borders of the Republic. Then the "Brits" will be out of Ireland at last. Or will they?

In the last century Giuseppe Mazzini, the great Italian prophet of nationalism, was not impressed by Irish apostles of the creed. He observed that the Irish did not seek any "distinct principle of life or system of legislation derived from native peculiarities and contrasting radically with English wants and wishes." In 1905 the Irish nationalist writer D.P. Moran was more acid: "There are certainly some traits to be found in Ireland which stamp her as a distinct race even yet, but they characterize her torpor and decay rather than her development." He added that if Ireland could not become bilingual it might just as well accept the historical fact that it was "West British." It is an amusing irony that the 19th-century Celtic revival, spurred in Ireland by Douglas Hyde, was actually founded in England by the poet Matthew Arnold. Always a middle-class academic exercise, it never took root in Ireland, where the use of Gaelic has become largely a ritual. Gaelic as the common speech of the Irish was wiped out by the 19th-century famine, surviving only in remote areas of the West, now called the Gaeltacht. This is itself a species of linguistic museum where English is spoken as much as Erse.

Celtic culture thus has less to do with Ireland today than Norman French culture has to do with both the United Kingdom and Ireland. After centuries of intermingling, the British and Irish are ethnically identical. For more than two hundred years the high culture of Ireland, from literature to architecture, has been predominantly British in its expression. As long ago as the 18th century Dublin was the second city of the British empire, and is today in many ways *more* British than some of the great conurbations of the United Kingdom. As the present troubles have shown, the political interests of Ireland and Britain are pretty well inextricable. Aside from mutual prejudice, regional accents, and the sectarian divide, there is little to separate Ireland and Britain except the width of the Irish Sea and the rituals of government. And as Mazzini predicted more than a hundred years ago, these rituals too are British. In the most profound sense Ireland has hardly separated from Britain at all. As a non-British entity the Republic is more of a notion than a nation. Unification would mean not the recovery of something old, but the expansion of that notion to make something new, or the illusion of something new.

No one, however, should make the mistake of underestimating the power of either prejudice or a political notion. On the first score nothing is more likely to provoke angry disagreement from a "Brit" or an Irishman than the suggestion that they are in any way alike. The British cliché-Irishman is a drunken, devious, blockheaded, and probably rather unhygienic bog-trotter who is priest-ridden, henpecked, lazy, breeds like a rabbit, and is prone to sing mawkish tenor songs about the ould sod, especially in his cups. He is also an irredeemable liar and hypocrite, imbued with a lethal Fenian hatred of the British. There is about as much truth in this as in the Irishman's bromide-Briton who is aseptic, coarse, brutal, arrogant, cunning but stupid and totally insensitive, unmusical, "Saxon," joyless, fundamentally irreligious and given to perversion, especially flagellation and homosexuality. He too is a liar and a hyprocrite and regards the Irish as scum. It is not the best material for weaving the tie that binds, even if the real differences between the two are less extreme than, say, between an upstate New Yorker and a native of Biloxi, Mississippi.

The political notion is the most poignant factor because it contains a paradox. To recover their rights as Englishmen, Americans severed themselves from England, and were never so British as when they did that. The Irish case is not quite the same, because Irish nationalism has always contained a dash of French revolutionary Jacobinism, which is essentially destructive of freedom while paying lip service to the Rights of Man. This is the strain which survives in the terrorist groups of Ulster today. It has never been representative in Ireland and is not now. That is why the Irish people accepted at first a separation from Britain that was formally incomplete, and in some respects still is. (For example, there is still no immigration control between the two countries. Irish citizens resident in the UK may work without special permission and legally vote in British elections.) Northern Protestants shored up their privileged position with a powerful notion that they shared in one of the greatest empires in the world. The wonder is not that the Republican Irish were unable to break it, but that they succeeded in reducing it to the size of a mere six counties. This does indeed violate the arbitrary postulate that "Ireland is One," and so frustrates and angers nationalists. But there is nothing inherently wrong or unjust in that. As Americans should know, there is no necessary symmetry between geography and a political notion.

What has been abominably unjust and cruel is the treatment of Ulster's Catholic minority. This has given emotional appeal and plausibility to irredentism among the Catholics, and to Republican claims for the annexation of the North. But these are no more "just" than German claims of a generation ago to the Sudetenland, or, say, an American claim to Saskatchewan if some minority there should ask for annexation and be badly treated for it.

But notions also die. Deprived of their imperial citizenship, Northern Protestants have now tried to maintain their ascendancy under a cloak of democracy which is threadbare even in the limited context of Ulster, because it means in practice the tyranny of a majority. This does not accord with the Western sense of democracy and has made the Protestants unpopular in the United Kingdom. Once the iniquity of their rule was exposed and forced into the public gaze, there might have been a chance of gradual (if reluctant) acceptance of reform and the real participation of Catholics in the political life of the province. Terrorism has not brought these things closer but pushed them further away—which is naturally part of the terrorists' deliberate intention.

So we find Yeats's house of the starling empty indeed, or rather filled with confusion. In Ulster a bellowing demagogue marches his Protestant goons up the hill and marches them down again, while the armed terrorists who are his avatars engage in lethal shadow play, egged on by their vicariously thrilled, ignorant, and bigoted American rooting section. The real context of it all is the

United Kingdom and Ireland together, where traditional political notions are under attack from Jacobin fascists on the Left and neo-Nazis on the Right, feeding like maggots on a rotting economy while striving to aggravate its discontents. In the United Kingdom, pressure groups spurn an older consensus of balance and careful progress, allowing little patience or time for the organic movement of democratic change. Demands for solutions in the form of theatrical or sudden gestures are loud both in parliament and on the streets, and they are redoubled by the squawks of concerned but ill-informed people abroad.

The people are right to see a danger in Ulster, but wrong to suppose that it lies in British "inflexibility," i.e., the refusal of the government to appease the terrorists and/or "unify Ireland." The enormous expense of Ulster—a major burden even for the United Kingdom—plus a mass of frightened and bellicose Protestants would in the present recession seriously destabilize the Republic, which is why its government wants none of it. At the same time the shock to the sovereignty of the United Kingdom, from a government seen to cave in before an unpopular and unrepresentative insurrection, would give a strong boost to separatists there, and to political extremists on both wings: the Right would be fortified by outrage and the Left by a scent of possible victory. Without a dramatic fall in unemployment and some surging improvement in the economy (neither of which is likely), there would be a chance (an off-chance perhaps, but a chance) of disturbance in Britain following such a withdrawal, in which extremists would find the opportunity of moving from talk to action, with some prospect of success.

But the people of the British Isles are resilient. With a modicum of luck and (if patience is in abeyance) stubbornness, and with less international kibitzing, their traditions may well survive economic misfortune and the revanchist hatreds which have so corrupted the politics of Northern Ireland. If the pall does lift and the industries of Britain and Ireland pick up again, sectarian differences can come to have less force than they have had in the workless ghettos of Ulster, and in the stultified agricultural backwater which Southern Ireland once was. In the North, with more for Catholic and Protestant to get and spend, and with a more active British interest in the rights of Catholics, the border may one day seem less of a threat, confounding the conventional wisdom which sees Ulster as an "intractable problem" not to be solved, but only dissolved from time to time in blood. Eventually the Republic may indeed spread its notion to the shores of Derry, Antrim, and Down, with Belfast and Londonderry still as British as Dublin is now. But even if that does not happen and the ritual separation of North and South remains (for like the separation of Britain and the Irish Republic it is just that: a ritual), the need to survive in a fiercely competitive world must inevitably push together the interests of the British and the Irish.

Whatever the dreams of the terrorists (and their friends in the United States), the logic of the past 800 years is not for them but against them. This period has seen, not a continual struggle to separate, but a gradual and inexorable merging of interests and peoples in these islands. As the Celts, with their language and culture, replaced an older people, so the Celts in their turn have been replaced; their world is gone, and no amount of rhetoric, historical fantasy, gunfire, or gelignite can bring it back now, If the people of the British Isles are divided for the time being by prejudice and abstractions, the division is still not as deep or as wide as some would like to make it. Such political wounds can be healed by necessity, and by notions which are less mean and parochial than those which made them. Despite the old grudges and the idealism perverted into malice, despite the bloodshed, despite the stupid, superstitious wrangling by Paisley and others over matters of faith, a real possibility may yet exist for Britain and Ireland to build in the empty house of the stare, welding in time another sort of union—stronger, more balanced, more enduring. Sooner or later this possibility must be faced, even by those who dedicate their lives to destroying it. For the rest of us it is something to hope for at a time when high hopes are in very short supply.

II. THE MAZE

EDITOR'S INTRODUCTION

In William Butler Yeat's play, *The Threshold,* quoted by Denis Donoghue in the first selection in this section, the character Seanchan (pronounced Shanahan) has a fallout with his monarch, King Guaire, and proceeds to starve to the death on the king's doorstep. As the king explains, "he has chosen death: refusing to eat or drink, that he may bring disgrace upon me" in "there is a custom, an old and foolish custom" whereby if a man starves himself to death on his enemy's doorstep he will bring disgrace forever upon that enemy. The story from which Yeats took his play is an old one, and whether it represents history or folklore or some murky combination of both is no longer clear, yet it has had a profound effect upon the Irish imagination. Fasting until death is an acceptable—not to speak of time-honored—form of extreme social or political protest, albeit not always a successful one. In 1920, the death by starvation of Terence MacSwiney had an impact on Anglo-Irish public opinion and helped to bring about the setting up of what was the Irish Free State, now the Republic of Ireland. But in the 1940s, the Irish government allowed several dissident patriots to die without stirring much fuss. In 1980, a group of IRA prisoners in Belfast's Maze prison undertook a fast that was stared down by Margaret Thatcher, Britain's Prime Minister. The next attempt, in early 1981, had a different outcome, culminating in the death by voluntary starvation of ten young men. Their goal was not primarily to bring disgrace upon Great Britain, although they surely had that in mind too, but to win status as political prisoners rather than as common criminals. This section is concerned with the issues surrounding these events.

The Maze hunger strike was not the first action taken by the imprisoned IRA men to attain political-prisoner status. Their first strategy was "going to the blanket," in which they refused to wear prison clothes and dressed only in the blankets issued to them by prison authorities. To make their point more forcibly, they declined the use of the chamber pots supplied them and instead smeared the walls of their cells with their own excrement. It was only when these tactics left their jailors unmoved that they resorted to the hunger strike.

The first selection in this section, "The Hunger Strikers" by Denis Donoghue, reprinted from the *New York Review of Books*, delves back into Irish history and folklore to point out that hunger strikes and fasts to the death have an ancient fascination for the Irish and ties it into the present situation.

In the second selection, Jack Holland describes the horror of life "on the blanket." His article is reprinted from *Commonweal*. The third article, by Robert Ajemian in *Time*, poignantly portrays what it is like to starve to death and why the IRA men do it. The fourth selection, an editorial from *America*, by the Reverend Joseph O'Hare, attacks British intransigence in compromising on minor issues, arguing that so doing prevents "the peaceful resolution of Northern Ireland's tragic dilemma."

The final report by *Time* brought the welcome news that the strike had finally come to an end.

THE HUNGER STRIKERS[1]

Everybody knows that ten men have starved themselves to death in the Maze Prison near Belfast in the past few months, but the reasons for those deaths are not universally understood.

On June 13, 1972, leaders of the Provisional IRA invited William Whitelaw, secretary of state for Northern Ireland, to discuss the possibility of making peace. The invitation was publicly rejected, but a conversational line was held open, mainly because John Hume of the Social Democratic Labour Party acted as mediator. Within two weeks a truce was effected. The British government agreed to five demands: 1) the prisoners would have the right to

[1] Article by Denis Donoghue. *New York Review of Books*. 28:29-31. O. 22, '81. Reprinted by permission. Copyright © 1981 Nyrev, Inc.

wear their own clothes; 2) they would not be required to do "penal labor"; 3) they would have the right to associate freely with their colleagues within their own prison area; 4) they would receive certain educational and recreational facilities; and 5) prisoners who had lost remission of sentence because of their protesting behavior in prison would have it fully restored. In return, the IRA agreed to stop its campaign of violence.

The agreement was brief. The truce ended on July 9, mainly because the situation involving the British Army, the IRA, and the Loyalist Ulster Defence Association was too confused to be contained for long. But "special category status" had been conceded, if only as a matter of expediency. When the truce ended, the British government let the concession persist, but it was soon clear that Whitelaw and his Labour successor Merlyn Rees had made a blunder. The British had achieved nothing, and they had acknowledged, in effect, that the IRA prisoners were not ordinary criminals but political prisoners.

In 1973 and 1974 a new policy was ordained: the IRA was to be confronted and defeated by the army, the normal work of security was to be taken over by the police and the Ulster Defence Regiment; acts of violence by the IRA were to be treated as ordinary crimes. The report issued by Lord Gardiner on January 30, 1975, concluded "that the introduction of special category status was a serious mistake." On November 4, 1975, Merlyn Rees announced that special category status would end on March 1, 1976: any prisoner sent to the Maze Prison after that date would be treated as an ordinary criminal. The five demands were made again.

Of course it is an embarrassment to the British government to be reminded that what they now regard as matters of principle were treated by their predecessors as negotiable. The present government's attitude is: we won't make the same mistake twice. It has also become clear to the government that the five demands are merely ostensible, and that the real cause of the hunger strike is elsewhere. It is naïve to think that the prisoners in the Maze are starving themselves to death to improve the conditions of daily life for their colleagues. Conditions in the Maze are already far easier than in most other prisons. There has been some talk of humanitarian considerations that the British government is urged to take into account, but the talk is wild. Cruelties are no longer practiced in the Maze. The prisoners, in fact, have not complained on humanitarian grounds; they have not protested about food, visiting hours, or any other empirical conditions which might be improved. The issue is special category status, though the phrase is no longer used.

But why are the prisoners (both the IRA and the smaller but even more violent Irish National Liberation Army) so insistent upon special category status or political status? It is not that they feel morally superior to the ODCs (ordinary decent criminals). In the event of amnesty, all political prisoners would at once be released, whatever their crimes. But the larger reason is that the IRA leaders are determined to take possession of the entire Republican tradition from the Rising of 1798 to the Fenians and the Men of Easter Week in 1916.

Irish education has a bearing on this matter. Teachers in Irish Catholic schools, in the North and the South, have until recently taught their pupils that the history of Ireland is one story and one only, the determination of the Irish people to get rid of the British presence in Ireland. In every generation, according to this interpretation, there has been a revolt; a small, heroic group has risen to drive the British out of Ireland. The revolt has been put down, but the spirit of the revolt has lived on. And in 1916 the spirit triumphed at last. Against British power and native ridicule, the heroes became martyrs. . . .Those whom the Irish ridiculed were now seen for the heroic figures they had always been. So the freedom of Ireland was at last achieved, but only in part. Lloyd George conspired with Sir Edward Carson to keep six northern counties permanently under British control, with a Protestant parliament for a Protestant people. There is still, then, a revolution to be fought, the last Rising, which will complete the struggle of 1916.

So we come back to the Provisional IRA. The Provisionals want political status so that they can present themselves as the legitimate heirs to the great Republican tradition. Until very recently most people in Ireland have regarded them as nothing of the kind. In the South, successive Irish governments have repudiated the IRA leaders, and rejected their claim to be the true heirs of the Men of 1916. Irish governments have taken the position that unity is still the aspiration of the Irish people, but that it is to be achieved by peaceful means and with the consent of all; it is not to be sought down the barrel of a gun or with the detonator of a bomb. So the Provisionals have been disowned, and are regarded as usurpers of a noble tradition. . . .

I speak of governments and, on the whole, of citizens. Support for the IRA comes and goes in Ireland. When they bombed the Abercorn Restaurant in Belfast in 1972 and injured many innocent people, they lost much of what support they had at the time. But people who are not the victims of such violence have a way of forgetting it. Support for the IRA also comes from America, where many Irish-Americans have grown up on the legends of heroic Ireland. And there are many people in Ireland who feel subliminal kinship with violence as a political means. Most people here are content to live with the common bourgeois life, but there are some who have residual feelings for a nationalism construed as militant and Republican. . . .

These are the feelings to which the provisionals appeal. In the Maze, the leaders have had time to prepare the current phase of their campaign. What they seek is to have themselves accepted as the only legitimate heirs to the true Republican tradition; accepted as soldiers, heroes, rather than as terrorists. Strictly speaking, at this moment the IRA is not in conflict with Britain or the British government; the declared conflict is merely nominal. The real conflict is with those Irish people who regard the IRA as perverts, corrupters of a great tradition. The Provisionals have only one aim at the moment: to compel the Irish people to acknowledge them as their true, legitimate sons.

The IRA can hardly hope to achieve this aim by force of argument, definition, and reason. They must transcend the terms of any such discourse. The only way to do that is by taking some morally intimidating course of action, something that requires courage, passion, and selflessness. Discourse can only be transcended by action: inside a prison, action can only take a symbolic form, all the more potent for being irrational and exorbitant. There is no gesture more compelling than the hunger strike, and ideally the hunger strike until death.

It seems to me fair to conclude that the H-block hunger strikes have nothing to do with conditions in the Maze, and everything to do with the IRA's claim to be the only true descendants of our Republican martyrs. . . .

If this is so, it must be conceded that the IRA campaign has already been extraordinarily successful. The several deaths by hunger have made "the damnable question" of Ireland news again. They have intimidated the Irish government into a whirl of misjudgments, including the foolish demand that President Reagan exert pressure upon Mrs. Thatcher to "resolve" the situation. The deaths have exacerbated the relation between the governments of Britain and Ireland, a relation not at all helped by Governor Carey's predictable delineation of Mrs. Thatcher as "implacable, obstinate, and stubborn." The well-meaning Social Democratic Labour Party has been knocked out of the political scene, at least for the time being. The deaths have also induced, in the leaders of the Catholic Church in Ireland, something close to hysteria and the folly that accompanies it. The relation between politics and discourse has been broken. And all this has been achieved by the carefully planned deaths of men who have shown that they regard the deaths of other people as casual events.

This much is clear. Many peaceable people in Ireland, who would like to see Ireland united but would not break anyone's head to achieve it, have now accepted, apparently, that the IRA hunger strikers, by dying, have transformed their cause. The text regularly quoted to endorse this attitude in W. B. Yeats's poem "Easter 1916." The poem tells of ordinary, inconsequential people, including one, "a drunken, vainglorious lout," who were transformed by their Republican dream and by its "excess of love" until they died. In another poem, Yeats wrote of "all that delirium of the brave," and he was ready to find, in what they did, delirium and self-bewilderment to the pitch of frenzy.

But it makes no difference. What remains, in many people, is a feeling that these men, and now the IRA and the INLA hunger strikers, have transformed their lives by the way in which they willed their deaths. Bobby Sands's death by hunger has achieved what he could never have achieved by his prowess with a gun. And it has been achieved not by reason or argument but by the primi-

tive force of a symbolic act. The point of a hunger strike in the
Maze is to ensure that the particular death will have the aura of
sacrifice: a sacrificial death can then be represented as having
transfigured the life it ended and the cause it served.

The hunger strike is a weapon of extraordinary potency in
Ireland, where there is a long tradition to enhance it. In one of
Yeats's plays Seanchan starves himself on King Guaire's thresh-
old, and at one point the king says:

> He has chosen death:/ Refusing to eat or drink, that he may bring/
> Disgrace upon me; for there is a custom,/ An old and foolish custom, that
> if a man/ Be wronged, or think that he is wronged, and starve/ Upon
> another's threshold till he die,/ The common people, for all time to
> come,/ Will raise a heavy cry against that threshold,/ Even though it be
> the King's./

When Terence MacSwiney died in Brixton Prison on October
25, 1920, that being the seventy-fourth day of his hunger strike,
he gave Republicans a weapon they already knew how to use. A
hunger strike forces ordinary people to feel guilty. They are alive,
the hunger strike is dead or dying, so he has the moral advantage.

In practical terms, hunger strikes in Ireland have rarely
achieved their immediate object. De Valera's government let Jack
McNeela die after fifty-five days, and Tony d'Arcy after fifty-two
days, on hunger strike in 1940, and Sean McCaughey after thirty-
one days in 1946. Liam Cosgrave's coalition government of 1973-
77 was unanimous, according to Conor Cruise O'Brien's recent
account of it, in facing down a serious hunger strike in Portlaoise
Prison. But it remains true that an IRA man's death by hunger
provokes in many people feelings of shame and outrage, and certainly does much to sustain the tradition of Republican violence.
Many people feel that a cause is transfigured when someone has
died for it, all the more so when he has chosen his death.

The present position is that that the British government has
announced, as a matter of principle, that it will not treat the Republican prisoners as political: their crimes are to be regarded as
secular, not spiritual. It is widely thought that Mrs. Thatcher's
hatred of the "men of violence" was rendered definitive by the terrorists' murders of the Conservative spokesman on Northern Ireland Airey Neave and Lord Mountbatten. In any case she is not

going to concede the five demands. One or two of them, perhaps; clothing is no longer a real issue, and the question of work can be fudged to some extent. But so long as the prisoners insist on the five concessions as a whole, there is no room for movement.

Besides, Mrs. Thatcher is not under any great international pressure on the matter. In the Maze, the Republican leaders have problems. When Owen Carron of Sinn Fein, the political wing of the IRA, was recently elected MP for Fermanagh/South Tyrone, several parents of the prisoners demanded that he take over the H-block issue and release the hunger strikers from their bond. Carron refused, on the grounds that the hunger strikers must continue to be seen, all over the world, as willing to die for their cause. But many of the parents remain dissatisfied, and some have called in the prison doctors and taken their sons off the hunger strike. There has been an arrangement between the IRA and the INLA by which the INLA would supply one hunger striker for every three supplied by the IRA. The INLA has only twenty-eight prisoners on the protest, compared to the IRA's 380, so the arrangement can't last for long. It is possible that the INLA will back out of its commitment and let the IRA go the rest of the way alone.

Carron's refusal to let the hunger strikers give up their fast was probably a mistake. It was not his decision, however: he is merely a puppet, the brain of the movement is the Sinn Fein leader Gerry Adams. But Adams, too, has made blunders. Carron was elected specifically and solely on the H-block issue. Adams could have presented Carron's victory as showing that "the common people" wanted to see the struggle carried beyond the Maze into the world at large, with Carron speaking on radio and TV. It would have been possible then to end the hunger strike and represent Carron's election as the next phase of the crusade. Adams chose otherwise. He evidently concluded that the strike still carries an emotional charge worth the cost. My own sense of the matter is that he is wrong. The Irish government, having blown hot, is blowing cold. Garret FitzGerald, the prime minister, now regards the IRA leaders as bearing, far more than Mrs. Thatcher, responsibility for the deaths. And the Catholic bishops are now emphasizing the futility of the hunger strike rather than Mrs. Thatcher's alleged intransigence in dealing with it. But even if the hunger strikes were to end tomorrow, it would not mean peace in Northern Ireland. The strike will be replaced by new intensity with the gun. Many Armalite rifles can be bought with the $250,000 collected during the last six months by Noraid, the IRA's support group in the U.S. . . .

THE MEN ON THE BLANKET[2]

They were aged twenty-one and twenty-two, as I afterwards learned, serving ten and twelve years respectively. When the cell door opened they both looked frightened and looked anxiously at us for a moment. They were pallid and naked except for a blanket draped over their shoulders. They stood silently, fear hardening into defiance, I felt, as we looked at the cell.

It was covered with excrement almost to the ceiling on all four walls. In one corner there was a pile of rotting, blue molded food and excrement, and the two boys had evidently been using bits of their foam rubber mattress to add to the decor as we entered. There wasn't much of a smell but the light was dim and the atmosphere profoundly disturbing and depressing. I felt helpless and angry as I stood and looked at these appalling and disgraceful conditions, prevented by bureaucracy and by history from talking to two of my fellow human beings who had brought themselves and been brought to this condition of self-abnegation.

So wrote Tim Pat Coogan, the editor of *The Irish Press,* in his recently published book about prison conditions in Northern Ireland, *On the Blanket.* He is one of the few outside observers ever permitted to visit that section of Northern Ireland's Maze Prison known as H-Blocks 3, 4, and 5. There, for the last three years, between three hundred and four hundred prisoners, mostly members of the Provisional Irish Republican Army, have been resisting the attempts of the prison administration to treat them as criminals. They claim they are not ordinary criminals but political prisoners whose actions were motivated not by greed or murder-

[2]Article by Jack Holland, contributor to *Commonweal* and author of *Too Long a Sacrifice* (on Northern Ireland). 1981. *Commonweal.* 107:652-4. N. 21, '80. Reprinted by permission.

ous intent but by the political goal of driving the British out of Northern Ireland and creating a united Ireland.

Another observer allowed in to witness the conditions in the H-Blocks was Cardinal O'Fiaiach, the Catholic Primate of all Ireland. He issued a statement shortly afterwards in which he said:

> Having spent the whole of Sunday in the prison I was shocked by the inhuman conditions prevailing in H-Blocks 3, 4, and 5, where over three hundred prisoners were incarcerated. One would hardly allow an animal to remain in such conditions. The nearest to it I have seen was the spectacle of homeless people living in sewerpipes in the slums of Calcutta. The stench and filth in some of the cells, with the remains of rotten food and human excreta scattered around the walls, was almost unbearable. In two of them I was unable to speak for fear of vomiting.

The cardinal's visit was in July 1978, when many of the prisoners had already been on the protest for eighteen months. Now, two years later, the British are still refusing to concede to the prisoners' demands to be treated as political not criminal offenders; and the prisoners are steadfastly refusing to wear prison clothes, do prison work, or in any way accept the status of common criminals. The resulting stalemate has produced the toughest problem the British government has had to cope with in its recent troubled administration of Northern Ireland. Most recently some of the prisoners have escalated their protest with a hunger strike. A hunger strike, combined with the horrendous squalor in which the prisoners live, carries the real possibility of a number of deaths, which in turn would only lead to more widespread and embittered violence throughout Northern Ireland.

The history of England's relationship with Ireland is in one very important sense a history of prison protests like the one currently taking place in the H-Blocks. As long as the Irish have resisted the colonialization of their country by England, imprisoned members of Irish terrorist groups have fought to have themselves acknowledged as political, not criminal prisoners. And England, of course, has resisted such an acknowledgment, which would be tantamount to admitting that there is a justifiable cause for struggle, for violence.

Occasionally, however, the British have made concessions to Irish prisoners which amounted to such an acknowledgment. In May 1972 a group of imprisoned Provisional IRA men went on a hunger strike to demand "political status"; this demand entailed that the prison authorities recognize the prisoner's right to wear his own clothes, to associated freely with other imprisoned members of his organization, to refuse to do prison work, and to receive extra visits and extra food parcels regularly. In 1972 the Provisional IRA were at the peak of their strength; their hunger-striking members were near to death when the government conceded, afraid that the security forces would be unable to contain the upsurge in violence expected if they died. Political, or "Special Category" status, was granted to the Provisionals (and, incidentally, to the jailed Protestant loyalist terrorists).

Four years later a Labor government abolished such privileges for any prisoner convicted of a crime after March 1976. From then on all prisoners, regardless of motivation, or membership in any terrorist guerrilla group, were to be treated like ordinary criminals. (The British referred to the latter as "O.D.C.'s": Ordinary Decent Criminals.) The labor government was attempting to characterize the violence in Northern Ireland as nothing other than gangsterism. Its overall policy, known as "Ulsterization," was intended to dispel the view that the problem was a political one. It was a strategy aimed at giving back more and more security responsibility to the largely discredited Northern Ireland police. And, after all, it was only appropriate that the police deal with "criminals."

The government's response to anti-H-Block protests is in line with this policy. British authorities point out with great emphasis that the prisoners are convicted murderers, bombers, bank robbers, and so on. The current figures show that the protesting prisoners have been responsible for some 50 murders, 35 attempted murders, 108 explosive offenses, and 80 firearms offenses. The authorities also claim that the conditions the prisoners endure are self-inflicted in the sense that they stem from their refusing to cooperate and they could at any time alleviate their suffering by cooperating. Any criticism of British behavior towards the protesters is met by these rejoinders.

However, when considering the government position it is well to remember several factors. The nature of the offense is hardly an argument against claims of "political" status. If it were, one would have to deny the legitimacy of violence as a method of political change under any circumstance. Of course, a government does do this when violence is directed against its organs. But this is a tactic within the realm of propaganda and should not be mistaken for a universal moral principle.

The authorities can also be questioned from another angle, a purely legal one that looks not to the nature of the offenses so much as to the nature of the forensic methods used to obtain convictions. The *Sunday Times* of London published figures in 1977 which showed that over 90 percent of those tried in Northern Ireland courts during the mid-1970s were convicted; of those, over 80 percent were convicted on the strength of confessions alone. This compares with a rate in normal United Kingdom courts of between 50 and 60 percent. I say "normal" because the Northern Ireland courts are special courts; they are non-jury courts where judgment is delivered by a single judge under special legislation known as the Emergency Provisions Act, made law in 1973. Under this legislation, provisions allowing for the admissibility of statements are much less strict than the provisions existing in English common law. In other words, the law has been specially arranged in Northern Ireland so that confessions can become acceptable evidence with an ease which has alarmed lawyers and led to several inquiries. Amnesty International in 1977, and a British committee in 1978, found that brutalilty was used regularly to obtain confessions which in turn led to convictions.

The special courts, the special legislation, the special methods used to obtain confessions, and the special concessions made to allow those confessions as evidence, point to a special situation which is not an ordinary criminal one. This alone would tell the world that the British government is not being candid or even consistent in its arguments that the Provisional IRA are just ordinary criminals and therefore not deserving of "special" i.e., political, status.

As to the conditions the prisoners endure, they can be described as self-inflicted only if one accepts the contention that passive resistance is a form of self-imposed suffering and, therefore, that the authorities are not to blame for the miseries endured by the protesters who use this method. (When Gandhi's followers, pursuing their program of satyagraha in South Africa, lay down in front of trains to protest the exploitation of their fellow Indians, would they have been accused of self-inflicted death—suicide— had they been killed?)

Resistance to the Ulsterization policy has been passive in the prisons. It began when Provisional IRA prisoners refused to wear prison clothes. The authorities retaliated by removing the mattresses and beds from the cells as well as any reading material. All that was left in the cell was a chamber pot until 8:30 p.m. when mattresses were returned. The prisoners claim that when the wardens came around with trolleys to pick up the slops in the morning they dumped the full chamber pots over the cells. The prisoners refused to clean up and began throwing the excrement out the cell windows. These were boarded up. So the prisoners began to daub it on the walls of the cells. "We had to put it somewhere so it was better on the walls than the floors," Coogan quotes one ex-prisoner as saying. The cells are power-hosed a few times a month. The prisoners dread these as they claim they are beaten when moved from the cells during the cleaning operations.

Prisoners are kept locked in their cells twenty-four hours a day naked except for a blanket wrapped around them (hence the term "blanketmen"). Sunday Mass is the only chance they have of getting out for an hour or so. Visits are restricted to one a month. But even these have become a source of anxiety because of the kind of examination the prisoner must endure before and after each visit. He is hauled upside down so that his back passage can be probed with long tweezers, or he is made to squat naked over a mirror for the same purpose. Many are so humiliated by this that they prefer not to have the monthly visit at all.

There are further humiliations. The prison orderlies (prisoners themselves) are responsible for much of the day-to-day running of H-Blocks. All the orderlies are convicted Protestant terrorists in jail for serious crimes—including murder—against Catholics. The protesting prisoners are Catholics and completely vulnerable to the animosities of their sworn enemies.

Outside, the reaction has been far from passive. Republican terrorist organizations have murdered twenty wardens over the last few years. There have been numerous protest marches throughout Ireland. Statements have been made by the Catholic church, liberal politicians, human rights organizations, left-wing Labor members of parliament and U.S. members of Congress, calling for concessions from the British government and asking that it recognize the prisoners' claims. Most recently Daniel Berrigan visited Belfast with a delegation of clergy and attempted to visit the H-Blocks but was refused. After he was denied permission he said: "Clergy are supposed to have access to prisons, so clearly these prisoners are a special case. We wonder if it is because they want the truth hidden of the inhuman treatment these prisoners are suffering."

In September a group of ex-prisoners who had been on the protest visited the United States illegally to publicize the awful conditions in the Maze, and in the women's prison in Armagh, where forty female inmates are now protesting the denial of political status. So far, however, the only sign of movement from the British government has been a partial concession to the prisoners' refusal to wear prison uniforms. The authorities offered to have civilian-type clothing supplied to all prisoners, political and otherwise, in Northern Ireland, but this concession was rejected by the protesters. At the end of October a number of the "blanketmen" began a long-threatened hunger strike; another 142 prisoners joined them a few days later, with every prospect of a further escalation of the protest.

The government refusal to acknowledge the political status of the prisoners is symptomatic of its general approach to Northern Ireland, treating it as a "law and order" problem while merely tinkering with temporary measures. Until the authorities abandon this narrow-sighted and politically dangerous view, which has helped create the present inhuman state inside the prisons, there is little chance of that crisis ending.

READY TO DIE IN THE MAZE[3]

The tray of food sits there, untouched. Every once in a while, the hunger striker steals a glance at it. After the first week, the servings seem enlarged to a ravenous man, the beans huge, the scones puffed up. His sense of smell is also more acute; he can detect the kind of food almost before it arrives. The breakfast tray waits until lunch, lunch stays until dinner, and dinner remains all night long. British authorities say they have the obligation to keep food always available. The prisoners consider the practice taunting and cruel.

But after two weeks, the war of nerves becomes irrelevant. The trays keep arriving, but by now the prisoners have lost their craving for food. The stomach cramps and pains recede and eventually disappear. The prisoners concentrate instead on their daily five pints of water. Now their only concern is whether they can hold down the water without retching. A small bowl of salt is provided for each prisoner, and he can sprinkle in as much as he wants. When the hunger strikes are far along, the prisoners ask for carbonated water and the British grant the request.

This is the world of the zealots, where Irish youth are willing to starve themselves for their cause of driving the British out of Northern Ireland. It is an astounding kind of sacrifice—a brutal, lingering death, full of hatred and martyrdom, so fanatical and Irish. The moment one striker dies, 50 volunteer to take his place. Tom McElwee, who died last week, wore a glass eye as a result of one of his own guerilla bombs. Behind him, at 55 days, Patrick Quinn, 29, had once slipped into unconsciousness. Big-bellied Michael Devine, 27, was at 48 days, gangly Lawrence McKeown, 24, at 41, and then, not too far behind, Patrick McGeown, 25, and Matt Devlin, 31, and more to come.

Street fighters from youth, terrorists half their lives, hardened and ruthless from years in prison, they are old at age 20. Because so many of the rebels, 406 of them, are locked in the H-shaped

[3] Article by Robert Ajemian. *Time.* 118:46-8. Ag. 17, '81. By permission from TIME, the Weekly Newsmagazine, Copyright Time Inc. 1981.

blocks of the Maze, they now believe they must win their war inside the prison, and that helps explain their astonishing defiance. But questions about them persist. Why are they so willing to starve themselves? How do they stand the pain? Are they afraid?

The intimate details of each death, spread eagerly from cell to cell, are well known to all the prisoners. Each time new volunteers are sought, Maze leaders review the awful effects of starvation. They want no false bravado and no dropouts. The prisoners stand silent against the cell-block doors, ears pressed to cracks in the framing, and listen to block commanders speaking in Gaelic to confound the guards, describe the ulcerated throats, the tooth fillings that drop out, the skin that turns so dry that bones break through, the inevitable blindness before death.

IRA leaders at first feared the idea of hunger strikes, believing the men would be unable to persist and would thus endanger the *esprit* of the movement. The longstanding question—Would starvation bring results?—was raised again early this year by prison leaders and debated for hours up and down the blocks. Some of the inmates spoke into the darkness and predicted glumly that the British would never yield. Such comments were usually met with silence. The men were asked to consider the proposal for one week and then volunteer if they felt ready to go.

A hundred offered to die. IRA commanders in the Maze, startled by the number, ordered the hunger strikes to begin. The volunteers quickly became heroes, paid special attention by the other prisoners, passed extra cigarettes, showered with support in the early days of stomach cramps. Poems were written to them and recited through the pipes and doors and shouted across the blocks.

Now the pattern of dying has become almost routine. After 21 days of no food, strikers are moved, past cheering cellmates, to continue their fast in the nearby prison hospital, a modern, one-story building where they are locked into individual rooms. Here they regain the status of prisoners who conform to regulations, and they are allowed to have visitors for one half-hour each day. The trays of food are always there. Radios are in each room and the strikers listen for special songs played for them by name by a sympathetic local station. But the men are even more interested in the hourly news, often interrupting conversation when they realize the program has already started, hoping, in the midst of dying, they will get word that the British have relented—that they can live. For two hours each evening, from 6 o'clock to 8, the hunger strikers are allowed to visit together in a small television room. Four or five gather at a time. After years alone in a cell, the men are fascinated by TV. The sudden appearance of their hated enemy, British Prime Minister Margaret Thatcher, sets them off into howls of outrage.

Prison officers say the hunger strikers undergo a drastic personality change when they leave the discipline of the blocks. They become far more civil, even amiable, finally speaking directly to the staff, asking and answering questions. They spend a great deal of time in bed, trying to preserve their strength. The staff puts sheepskin rugs in their beds to warm their bodies, now slowly turning colder. Although they refuse medication, the men do ask the nurses to give them liniment rubdowns to soften their parched skin. A barber comes in once a week to trim their hair and, if they are feeble, give them a shave. The prisoners are weighed daily and always anxiously demand to know the exact figure, then pass the word immediately to their waiting IRA comrades, who spread it everywhere. Joe McDonnell, 30, dropped from 196 lbs. to less than 100 before he died on July 8.

At 42 days, almost exactly, a nightmarish experience occurs. They have been thoroughly warned, and the prisoners await the moment with great alarm. They are struck by something called nystagmus, a loss of muscular control due to severe vitamin deficiency. If they look sideways, their eyes begin to gyrate wildly and uncontrollably, first horizontally and then vertically. The prisoners struggle to stare straight forward, even cupping their hands against the sides of their heads, but they cannot help themselves. Francis Hughes, 25, the second striker to die, even constructed cotton gauze blinders around his eyes.

Nystagmus also causes spells of constant vomiting and dizziness. The whole experience is terrifying and no amount of advance description can begin to prepare the strikers for the ordeal. When it ends, usually right on schedule after four or five days, they are enormously cheered up and for about a week go through a physical and psychological revival.

But now the end is not far off. Their speech is slurred, and they try not to talk because the sound of their own voices echoes in their heads. Their hearing is failing and visitors have to shout during normal conversations. They are slowly going blind. Even their sense of smell is fading.

Their families are with them often now and together they flash back to early memories and images. Francis Hughes, a folk hero inside the Maze long before his death, retained his needling, cheery nature to the end, lying in bed and singing rebel songs in a thin hoarse voice, his sad relatives gathered around him.

Their families usually are helpless. They sit beside the beds, haunted by doubts about whether or not to intervene. "A son is a son," said Bridie McTaggert, who had come to visit her brother, Kevin Lynch, 25, a couple of days before he died, "but my mother has to accept this." When families timidly suggest giving up the strike, sons turn their faces away or weakly hold up their palms asking them to stop. If mothers plead, some angry sons will order them out of the room and refuse further visits. Bobby Sands, 27, warned his mother he would never speak to her again if she interfered after he lost consciousness.

But a fortnight ago there finally was a break in that reluctant agreement by the families to accept the men's wishes. Catherine Quinn decided she could no longer obey such orders. When her son Patrick, 29, was unable to hold down water and fell unconscious, she defied him and had prison authorities take him to a nearby hospital and feed him intravenously. "He can't make a decision for himself any more," she said, "I want my boy to live." When Pat Quinn regains his wits, the cruel struggle between family and cause will continue.

Catherine Quinn's desperate boldness sent a wave of hope through hundreds of families who live in dread of the sudden news that their sons have volunteered to starve. When the name of the latest hunger volunteer, Liam McCloskey, 25, was announced last week, his parents protested to the IRA that their son had a chronic ear infection that could cause early death. They dared to express their indignation.

Nonetheless, some families are caught up in the cause even more than their sons. Hunger Striker Raymond McCreesh, 24, went about 50 days without food and one day wondered aloud to a member of the prison staff if a single glass of milk would violate his fast. After all, McCreesh said hesitantly, it was only liquid, like the five pints of water and salt he took each day.

The staffer was so unnerved by the questions that he rushed word to the prison governor who swiftly summoned members of McCreesh's immediate family. One of them pulled a chair close to the bed, for by now Raymond was partly deaf, and reminded the prisoner that he had made a pledge to his comrades. Then the relative alluded to the first hunger striker to die this year: "Remember, Bobby Sands is waiting for you in heaven." Raymond gave up asking for milk and died a week later.

The prisoners who support the strikers often remind each other bitterly that living may be worse than dying. The cause they cling to is far more compelling than anything in their bleak home neighborhoods. Instead, the prisoners have created their own society inside the Maze that enables them to continue the struggle. Each of the four wings in a block has a commander and an adjutant, and each block has an intelligence officer and an education officer. The inmates speak Gaelic; those who do not know the language are taught inside the prison. The entire hierarchy is run by a shrewd, tough commander, Brendan McFarlane, 25, who is serving 25 years for blowing up a pub and killing five civilians.

McFarlane and his staff keep a close eye on the guards, searching for some who have been imported from the south because they understand Gaelic. Prisoners try to trick guards who are suspect, making a shocking remark to them in Gaelic about killing their children. If they see as a flicker of response, they know. Ordinarily, prisoners never speak to the guards directly or even look at them. It is part of the endless psychological war.

Prisoners are ingenious about looking after themselves, rubbing their toenails and fingernails on the concrete to keep them short. Long letters printed on toilet paper in miniature handwriting are sneaked out by the hundreds. One inmate, John Thomas, swallowed a small cigarette lighter, intending to store it in his body for a couple of days. A metal detector picked it up and it was removed by a purgative.

Isolated in their cells, the men devise ways of passing items across corridors by stripping threads from cotton towels and attaching a button. Then they swing the button under the door until it intersects with another thread and button from across the hall. Once the link-up is made, the inmates pass small objects to each other. Another way of transferring such items as cigarettes is to tie them to the end of a towel or a trouser leg, and then swing them from one window to the next.

The Maze springs alive for the prisoners around midnight when the guards tend to be less alert and less in evidence. The perfect evening is when the air is still, without a trace of wind or rain. Prison leaders shout into the quiet darkness and their voices carry easily between the H-blocks separeted by about 100 ft. The men are called "scorchers," an anglicization of the Gaelic word *scairt,* for shout, and they fill the air with orders and questions and plain gossip. Sometimes they conduct quiz shows, asking questions about entertainment figures, geography, history. When someone wins, a cheer rises in the blackness.

But always, as life goes on in the Maze, the IRA men are inspired and haunted by those who are about to die. The fate of the hunger strikers dominates the prison. Guided by orders from outside the Maze McFarlane and his lieutenants still have a great deal of control over the prisoners and spend hours picking volunteers to replace the strikers who die. The leaders choose grit rather than physical strength, often quoting Bobby Sands, a small man who said of his own hunger experience, "The body fights back, sure enough, but at the end of the day, everything returns to the mind. If you don't have a strong mind to resist, you won't last."

The pressure from fellow prisoners is heavy. To volunteer to go on strike and then quit would be an overwhelming disgrace, roughly akin to the basic Irish horror of becoming an informer. One prisoner, Sean MacStiofain, at the time the No. 2 man in the IRA, started a hunger strike in 1972 and quit after 57 days. He was relieved of his command.

The will to endure is strong, almost maniacal. Sands, a cold, sullen man, turned on his bedside radio and listened with a faint smirk to news broadcasts of his own final hours. Even when the end is not far off, there are some lighter moments. Only days before he died, Kevin Lynch asked his family to bring him some cigars. He lay there, his body emaciated, his voice a whisper, blowing smoke toward the ceiling. The mother and girlfriend of Kieran Doherty, 25, were lifting his shrunken body for a rubdown when he almost slid from the bed; the prisoner kidded them about taking 24 hours off his life.

From start to finish, it is a mournful scene, prisoners in green pajamas and blue robes, shuffling around slowly, trying to stretch their fasts—and lives—as long as they are able. The British will not force-feed them. They claim that such an act amounts to personal assault and, besides, they say the doctors will not obey such orders. Hospital pathologists report that post-mortems reveal no single cause of death. Rather, the young bodies simply wither away. It is a terrible way to die, bodies slowly wearing out, time and faces blurring. The prisoners strengthen themselves from time to time by recalling the words of a famous IRA hunger striker, Terence MacSwiney, who fasted for 74 days in 1920 before dying. "It is not those who can inflict the most," said MacSwiney, "but those who can suffer the most who will conquer." British authorities, for their part, are convinced the Irish cannot continue indefinitely to sacrifice their young. "They just can't keep it up," says Humphrey Atkins, Secretary of State for Northern Ireland, a man who sounds as dogged as the H-blockers.

Rebel leader Gerry Adams, 34, recently spent an afternoon with the strikers in the Maze. They gathered in the TV room and, speaking only in Gaelic, Adams told them bluntly there was little chance of anything changing. If the strikers wanted to abandon their fast, he went on, they would not be scorned. They had already done more than could be asked.

The prisoners said they wanted to go on anyway. Adams then said he believed they would all very soon be dead. By his word, he seemed almost to be inviting them to break their fast. But they would have none of it. For a moment, they stared back at him in silence. So be it, the silence said.

HUNGER STRIKE ON H-BLOCK[4]

As the fast of seven prisoners in Maze prison near Belfast moved into its sixth week, a tragic conclusion appeared more and more imminent. Both sides—the British Government and the prisoners, supported by the Provisional Irish Republican Army—were locked in a duel to death. The British insisted that the prisoners must accept responsibility for their own condition and announced that prison officials would make no attempt, as they had in the past, to force-feed the hunger strikers. The very fact that there were seven men committed to the fast unto death made it less likely that any individual could be persuaded to cease his fast and break the strike. Whatever frail bonds had been woven between moderate Catholics and Protestants in Northern Ireland were strained to the breaking point as the churches were drawn into opposed positions according to denominational loyalties.

For propaganda purposes, the Provisional strategy appeared to be having its desired effect. Although both the political and religious leaders of the Catholics in Northern Ireland insist that the Provisionals do not enjoy wide support, the conditions in which the prisoners lived and the intransigence of the British on the question of what clothing the prisoners should wear has provoked widespread outrage among Catholics not only in Northern Ireland but also abroad.

Since 1976, when the British Government insisted that prisoners convicted of terrorist crimes were to be treated as common criminals, Republican prisoners in the notorious H-block section of Maze prison have refused to wear prison uniforms and "have gone on the blanket." Although access to H-Block has been severely restricted, several visitors, including Ireland's Roman Catholic primate, Cardinal Thomas O Fiaich, have testified to the increasing squalor in which the prisoners live. The British insist that the degradation of the prisoners is self-inflicted and therefore disclaim any responsibility for the shocking living conditions.

[4] Editorial by Reverend Joseph O'Hare. *America, National Catholic Weekly*. 143:361. D. 6, '80. Reprinted by permission.

The British refusal to consider Republican prisoners in any special category is based on the fear that any special treatment would thereby legitimize the terrorist activities of the Provisional IRA. British failure to recognize the historical and political roots of the violence in Northern Ireland has been one of the reasons why a workable solution to the conflict has not been realized. In the present instance, the British, by refusing to compromise, have been maneuvered into a position where the relatively trivial issue of what clothing prisoners should wear has been allowed to drive a wedge between those groups in both communities who have been working for a peaceful resolution of Northern Ireland's tragic dilemmas.

Some concessions from the British seemed to have been won when Cardinal O'Fiaich and Bishop Edward Daly of Derry persuaded officials to allow the prisoners to wear civilian clothing rather than prison uniforms. In effect, however, the British took back this concession, when they insisted that prison officials would issue the civilian clothing. Greater flexibility and greater courage, in withstanding the threats of Protestant extremists, on the part of the British Government, is necessary if further tragedy and violence are to be averted. Surely some prison reforms could be installed that would not necessarily legitimize the Provisional IRA but would realistically defuse an explosive tragedy.

THE STRIKE ENDS[5]

Two quite different developments took place last week that could ease both historic and recent tensions in Northern Ireland. The more dramatic came from Maze Prison, where at week's end Irish Republican militants announced that they were giving up their seven-month campaign of fasting that has left ten dead since it began last March. In Dublin, Prime Minister Garret FitzGerald launched a bold initiative to change the constitution of the

[5] Article from Time. 118:58.0. 12, '81. By permission from TIME, the Weekly Newsmagazine, Copyright Time Inc. 1981.

Irish Republic in ways that would make unification of the divided island more conceivable.

The statement from the prisoners was inevitable. Earlier, word spread that families of the final six fasting inmates would not permit their men to die. They were following the lead of four other families who intervened with Maze authorities to save prisoners' lives. Three other strikers decided to abandon the fast on their own. Richard McAuley, a leader of the Sinn Fein, the political arm of the IRA, has admitted that under such circumstances the hunger strike was placing "little or no pressure" on the British to yield to the prisoners' demands for political status, though the government of Prime Minister Margaret Thatcher had shown no indication of doing so in any case.

Meanwhile, Prime Minister FitzGerald was trying to make unification of the Republic and Ulster more attractive to Northern Ireland's Protestants, who have protested that they would be swallowed up in a predominantly Catholic state. FitzGerald proposed changing the Republic's constitution and laws to remove Catholic bias. He cited articles that claim jurisdiction over the whole island and ban divorce. FitzGerald is likely to have trouble getting his plan passed by the Dáil, since he leads a coalition that has only a two-vote margin. If approved, the constitutional amendments would have to be ratified by national referendum.

The Catholic Church made no response to FitzGerald's proposals last week, but they were hailed by leading Protestant clergymen in the Republic. In Ulster, Protestant firebrand Ian Paisley railed that FiltzGerald's plan would "in no way weaken our resolve never to come under Dublin rule." Catholic leaders gave the initiative a guarded welcome. Said Sean Farren, chairman of the predominantly Catholic Social Democratic and Labor Party: "Many changes, both in attitudes and in law, are needed if a meaningful agreement is to be achieved between the people of Ireland."

Prime Minister FitzGerald was trying to make one of the first and most fundamental changes—and betting his political career on it.

III. LIFE IN ULSTER

EDITOR'S INTRODUCTION

What is it like to live in Ulster today? There are certainly other parts of the world where, in the words of one letter quoted in the first selection in this section "there is always someone pointing a gun at you." So perhaps life in Belfast is not so different from life in other strife-torn cities such as Beirut or San Salvador or one of the occupied cities of Afghanistan. Still, Belfast is different, if only that the situation has been of such long duration and the hopelessness of it seems more ingrained.

One portrait of Belfast life is depicted in the first selection, subtitled "Letters from a Belfast Ghetto," by Jack Holland, reprinted from *The Nation*. Another, by John Conroy in the *New York Times Magazine* describes the restlessness and taste for violence that spills over on the young men, known as the "hoods" who have to grow up in this sort of climate. And finally, another facet of life in Ulster is pictured by Anthony Bailey in a report from *The New Yorker*.

LETTERS FROM A BELFAST GHETTO[1]

Well, Jack have you settled down in your new home, or do you miss old Belfast anymore? There is not much change here. The war is still going on and not getting any better. Two weeks ago they [the Provisional Irish Republican Army] burned the Greenan Lodge Hotel down, this week a few shops in the town and numerous other places. And to make matters worse, the firemen are out on strike. The shootings go on.

Your loving,
Mother

[1] Article by Jack Holland, Belfast poet and journalist; now free-lance writer in New York City. *The Nation*. 228:300-3. Mr. 24, '79. Reprinted by permission.

The date on the letter was November 11, 1977, shortly after I had moved to New York. The return address: Andersonstown Park South, part of Belfast's largest Catholic ghetto. The sender: my mother, a working-class women in her mid-50s, with five children and a husband out of work for the first time in his long life as a truck driver. The situation: Northern Ireland after ten years of civil crisis and guerrilla war. The prospects: pretty hopeless. At least once a month for the last ten years or so that I have lived away from home, the letter would arrive in my mailbox. For most of those years the letter has carried much the same message: the war goes on, things haven't changed. Only the list of the dead gets longer.

My mother is one of the people on whose behalf the war is supposedly being fought: One side—the IRA—claims to be fighting to defend her against the British; and the other—the British—asserts it is there to protect her from the terrorists. Ordinary people rarely have the opportunity to give their view of history, which is ironic since history affects them often more directly than anybody else. And what affects them become the details out of which history is made. When a mother cannot get down the street to shop for her family, or when a man cannot get to his job because of the violence, that is as much a fact of history as the fall of a government. (Indeed, in Northern Ireland facts such as these have, on two occasions since 1968, contributed to the fall of governments.) The people for whom these are facts of life—of everyday life—reveal through their feelings and experiences a barometer of the political crises. For a long time now the reading has remained steady at "Resignation," the result of the experience of a decade of continuous violence within a population approximately one-eighth that of New York City. There is little cause for hope. Early last year, a letter from my mother described the "prospects" for her, and for Northern Ireland in the year ahead:

The troubles here are not getting any better. In the last couple of days the IRA have shot and killed one member of the Ulster Defense Regiment [a locally recruited regiment of the British Army]. And this morning they booby-trapped another U.D.R. man's car as he was taking his two children to school. It blew up, killing him and his 10-year-old daughter and the wee baby that was in the back is critically ill. There was another shooting at the corner of Andersonstown Park, not far from our street.

A plainclothes policeman was passing in his car and they riddled the car. He is in hospital seriously wounded. Another policeman was shot down in York Road, and a woman who was passing at the time was shot dead in the cross fire. I could go on and on as each day brings a new tragedy. There seems to be no end to it. . . .

This letter was dated February 8, 1978. Two weeks later a series of bombs went off in a popular hotel outside Belfast called La Mon House, killing twelve people. The Provisional I.R.A., who claimed responsibility, apologized by saying it was a terrible mistake. A subsequent letter from my father indicated that, apologies or not, it had badly affected I.R.A. support. He wrote. "The La Mon House bombing was a terrible tragedy. It has turned a lot of people against them and the troubles in Belfast." Even hard-core supporters of the I.R.A. were disgusted at the senseless waste of human life.

But the history of Northern Ireland over the last ten years is a history of similar tragedies, now all indistinct parts of that bloody tapestry. Not only the I.R.A. but the British Army, the Northern Ireland Police and the assassins of the Protestant paramilitary organizations have all been guilty of outrages in Northern Ireland. Each new atrocity is soon thrown into the balance against the last one.

For the ordinary Catholics of Andersonstown, however, the violence is only one, if the most brutal, of the problems with which they have to cope. One of the most pressing is work, or the lack of it. Andersonstown is part of an area that has up to a 40 percent unemployment rate among men. Our family was considered fortunate in that my father, a truck driver, always had a job—that is, until 1975 when his company closed. My mother went to work to help support the family. She found a job in the canteen of a nearby electrical parts factory, which was brought into the area to try to alleviate joblessness. It offered 300 jobs. Over 3,000 men applied for them.

Though she often worked seven days a week serving and cleaning in the canteen, she never brought home more than the equivalent of $40. Last February she wrote in a paragraph, after the latest violent incidents were mentioned:

I have become one of the unemployed. We were all laid off work three weeks ago after 140 men in the factory lost their jobs. We weren't needed in the canteen. I miss the few extra pounds.

The company was losing money, and had to cut back its work force, abandoning its previous plans to give jobs to more than 1,000 Catholics from the area.

Fortunately, by this time there were only two of the five children in my parents' family still at home, attending school. The others were married and—apart from myself—all living in Andersonstown. None had jobs; all were more or less dependent on welfare checks. Unemployment has been a fact of life for Catholics since the Northern Ireland state was founded in 1921. The last ten years of civil rights struggle, social unrest and finally guerrilla warfare have not changed that. In fact, the figures for 1978 show that unemployment is at its worst since any time after World War II. Because of the still active discrimination in favor of Protestants in many areas of Northern Ireland's industry, those most drastically affected are the ordinary Catholic people of developments like Andersonstown.

Sectarian lines are clearly drawn in Northern Ireland, and neither Catholics nor Protestants will leave their own areas even to visit the others. This has been the cause of many problems for those families which, like my father's, are mixed. My father's father was a Protestant who married a Catholic. Some of their children, including my father, were brought up as Catholics, and some as Protestants. My father's eldest brother, William, is a Protestant. After the start of the troubles in 1969 he stopped visiting his Catholic relatives, whom he had till then seen regularly. For four years my father did not see him. Then, in 1973, my mother wrote to me of a chance meeting they had in downtown Belfast:

By the way, Jack, I thought you'd be interested to hear that your father met your Uncle William last week in the city center. He has had to move from his street because of the troubles, and now lives in a quieter area. But he says he's still scared to come to Andersonstown. He's just as frightened of his own side as he is of the IRA. But he promised as soon as the troubles ended he'd be up to see us. Isn't it awful the way your own family can't feel safe coming to see you now?

That was the summer of 1973. Nearly six years later the killings are still going on, and my father has seen his brother only once since—it took a death in the family to bring them together again—at the funeral of one of their sisters.

Sectarianism has split up communities, and broken families. It has not stopped short of killing those from its own side if they are seen to be friendly with the other side. But the main thrust of the sectarian violence has been directed against the Catholics. By far the greatest majority of those killed by sectarian attacks have been Catholics, and they outnumber Protestant victims by two to one. It is this, more than anything else, that has caused fear and dismay among Catholics since the Protestant assassination squads began operating in late 1971.

I was in England through most of 1972, and the letters I still have from that year recreate the terror experienced by so many Catholics, particularly in Belfast. One from my mother is dated June 1. Along with the letter was a press clipping of a report about the murder of a young Catholic, Gerard McCusker, whose sister my mother had met.

> I hope you are studying hard and do well in the tests. We have thought about you a lot recently, and we are glad you are out of Belfast. Anything can happen here now. We hear awful stories about what the Protestant gangs like the U.D.A. [Ulster Defense Association, the biggest of the Protestant terrorist groups] are doing to Catholics they catch. I enclose a report about wee Gerard McCusker from the Falls. He was murdered last week. I met his sister the other day. She was talking to someone in a shop about it, and was in tears. She says his body was all cuts and bruises. His wrists were broken and his hair was pulled out. His hands were tied with wire. He'd been beaten before being shot. The police say they have no clues to who did it. But everybody knows fine rightly it was the U.D.A. or the U.V.F. [Ulster Volunteer Force, the oldest of the Protestant paramilitary groups]. His body was found in the Shankill. People are afraid to go out at night. They say there's a madman roaming Belfast. Nearly all the women in the street are on tranquilizers. They won't allow their boys out at night. You're lucky to be out of it, son.

My mother, like most working-class women in Belfast, went on tranquilizers herself. She wrote to tell me disturbing news of how the assassinations were affecting the children. One of my sisters, Eileen, age 13 at the time, was badly upset:

Poor Eileen has nightmares lately. She can't sleep and is always getting up in the middle of the night to go downstairs to switch on the lights.
She says she's scared of the dark now. You know she saw a man being
shot dead outside her school? I'm taking her to the doctor tomorrow to
see if he can give her something to help her rest at night. . . .

Children are affected by the violence in many ways. In local
schools discipline has broken down. Attendance has fallen drastically, and teachers are at a loss to know how to enforce their will
on children who spent much of their free time rioting against
heavily armed soldiers, or who in some cases by their early teens
were training to shoot high velocity rifles and plant bombs. One
incident reflects the kind of atmosphere in which schooling had
to survive. In 1973 Thomas went to secondary school at the age
of 11. Shortly after he had started, my mother described an event
which left a big impression on the children:

Anyway, Thomas came home early today and told me that his school
had been taken over by the Officials [the other IRA faction, dominated
by Moscow-oriented Communists]. They were in class at about 11 o'clock
when they saw a group of young men coming into the corridors. They
were carrying rifles and wearing masks. They went into all the class-
rooms and ordered the teachers out; then they put them into a storeroom
and locked the door. Then the Officials went back into each classroom
and read statements to the children. Thomas said everybody thought it
was a laugh. He said he didn't remember much about the statement, except it was about history. They left the teachers in the storeroom for over
an hour and then gave the children the keys to the storeroom and told
them to let the teachers out whenever they liked. Then they left. Thomas
said that some of the boys didn't want to let the teachers out at all. But
they were afraid they might suffocate, so they opened the door. . . .You
never know what'll happen next in this place, do you?

There have been two developments over the past five years
which seemed to offer the chance of a way out of the morass. The
first was the more serious: the attempt to set up a government in
Northern Ireland in which Catholics would, for the first time in
the history of the state, share power with Protestants. The Power-
Sharing Executive took office in January 1974. Five months later
it was forced out by action of the largest Protestant paramilitary
group, The Ulster Defense Association. The U.D.A. organized a
series of intimidatory tactics which successfully kept thousands of
poeple from their jobs and controlled the flow of food and essential

services to the entire city of Belfast. The British Army did not intervene effectively. By the end of May 1974, the power-sharing government was brought to its knees and resigned. Ever since there has been a political vacuum in Northern Ireland which has not been filled. It was out of that vacuum, in 1976, that there came the second development: the Peace Movement. It was very different from the politically controversial assembly. In fact, it was motivated by the most uncontroversial of all demands, the demand for peace.

However, as the letters from my mother during that period show, this optimism or enthusiasm was not shared by all of Belfast's working-class women. About one month or so after the Peace Movement was launched I received this letter from home in answer to an inquiry:

How have you been keeping these last weeks? Thank God we are all well, and waiting to see what will happen next now the peace women have taken to the streets. No, Jack, I haven't joined in. In my eyes they are very well-intentioned but I don't think they can last. In some areas they are strong, but mostly the better-off places. In others, like the Lower Falls, the people don't want them. Your sister Eileen told me the other day that in her school the children of any women who are in the Peace Movement get beaten up by the other kids.

Anyway, I think they are in danger of getting carried away with themselves. Every time you switch on TV they are being interviewed. Do they think that by standing and praying and singing hymns that peace will fall from the sky? I think it just makes them feel good, but it won't change this place. If prayers would work, we would have had peace years ago. Don't you agree?

After the period of marching and praying stopped, and the movement tried to organize itself along practical lines, its problems began to emerge. It seemed that without the atmosphere of religious emotion, without the great gatherings, it was rapidly fading into the background while the violence continued as ever. When Betty Williams and Mairead Corrigan received the Nobel Peace Prize last year my mother again wrote about them:

Jack, you want to know my opinion about the Peace People now? I don't have much interest in them. You very rarely hear about them in Belfast. I think the movement is dying slowly. . . .I did hear that Betty Williams has left Andersonstown and went to live in the Malone Road.

The Malone Road is a wealthy middle-class district of Belfast, greatly resented by the ordinary people, both Catholic and Protestant, because of its apparent immunity from the violence and hardship which have always afflicted their lives. The story that Betty Williams has moved into a rich area has been a continuing rumor in the Catholic ghettos of Belfast. It is symptomatic of a feeling that the Peace Movement no longer is identified with the needs of the ordinary people. For them, going to live on the Malone Road is like moving to the Bahamas. (In fact, the Peace People have opened their headquarters in the Malone Road, which might help to explain the rumor.)

War numbs those it does not kill. Feelings that have to cope with violent death on a daily basis soon become exhausted—there is only so much tragedy and horror a person can deal with, whilst still going about his or her everyday life. In order to survive, they must withdraw from the tragedy, suppress the grief. But no one ever really forgets. For my mother, as for most of the people of Northern Ireland, the last decade has become a list of those they lost, the relatives, the friends, the neighbors; all victims of a war that is fought out in the front parlors of their homes, in their streets, in their bars, at their work places.

The next decade might well make that list as long again. They are all potential victims, wherever they are, or whatever they do. There is little hope for change. In an old letter, my mother put it like this:

Belfast is a terrible place. No matter where you go there is always someone pointing a gun at you.

The imponderables remain. Those who are determined to destroy the Northern Ireland state are still in arms. Those who are determined to defend it are ready to respond. And those who do not know or those who are now past caring, as usual make up the majority of the victims.

ULSTER'S LOST GENERATION[2]

The first killing Sean Nolan remembers took place about 1 o'clock of an August morning 12 years ago when police opened fire on the Divis Flats housing project in Belfast. Sean was 6 years old. He remembers mattresses against the windows of the family's flat and the noise of machine-gun fire. He crept under his bed and wept. Later he learned that his playmate Patrick Rooney had been killed when a bullet passed througth his head.

Today, Sean Nolan—his name has been changed so as not to incriminate him—is embarrassed to recount his childhood terror. He has seen more deaths, more shootings and many riots since then. He is part of a generation now coming of age in working-class, Roman Catholic districts in Northern Ireland that grew up throwing stones at police vans and army vehicles, taunting soldiers as they hauled off fathers and brothers in dawn raids. It is a generation without hope—with little prospect of employment and no stake in normal society. Many, like Sean, have taken to petty theft; they are known locally as the hoods. Northern Ireland is not a country consumed by war. The fighting for the most part has been limited to Catholic ghettos like West Belfast, and even in such pockets, there have been occasional small reminders over the past decade of a more peaceful time. Just a year ago, for example, members of the Royal Ulster Constabulary—at least 90 percent of whom are Protestant—were able to get out of their armored jeeps and patrol parts of West Belfast without being the targets of sniper fire or petrol bombs. And last fall, for the first time in years, Educational Welfare Officers began taking truant youngsters to court.

But any such developments have been swept away in the waves of anger since last May, when Bobby Sands became the first of the Irish Republican Army inmates in the Maze Prison to starve himself to death. As successive hunger strikers died, their

[2] Article by John Conroy, free-lance writer; written on an Alicia Patterson Fellowship in Belfast. *New York Times Magazine.* p 19+. Ag. 2, '81. Copyright 1981 by The New York Times Company. Reprinted by permission.

demands for a liberalization of prison rules refused, the Catholic populace became enraged, and riots flared.

At the center of the riots, as always, were the young hoods. They are afflicted with a very special bitterness. They are lawless, but with a moral code that accepts the disciplinary kneecappings meted out by the IRA. They are deeply apathetic, but they show a reckless courage, barreling through army checkpoints in stolen cars. And, in the view of some psychiatrists, they may actually have a lower incidence of mental illness than ghetto children in many other nations. The hoods of West Belfast are a dramatic illustration of the extraordinary adaptability of human beings under pressure.

Sean Nolan is 5 feet 6 inches tall, slim, a natty dresser with a crew cut. He comes from a family of 16, two of whom have been members of the IRA and have done time in jail for the movement.

Unlike many of his pals, Sean has not scarred himself with a homemade tattoo ("Mum" and "UTH"—short for "Up the Hoods"—are popular). He doesn't smoke, and he gets drunk only rarely; he sleeps 11 hours a day. By his own account, he has stolen 200 cars for the fun of it and has twice been shot at by the army in the process.

Sean's steady income is from the dole, which amounts to about $40 a week, of which he gives $30 to his mother for room and board. He supplements that with petty thievery. The most money he has ever had was $160, the proceeds from the sale of whisky and cigarettes he stole from a parked car last Christmas. "I sold them in Divis," he says, "Everybody dives for things in the flats."

Some 363,000 people live in Belfast, almost a quarter of the population of all of Northern Ireland. The central shopping area, patronized by Protestants and Catholics alike, is surrounded by tall, steel fencing. Every man, woman and child who enters is frisked. Divis Flats, a housing project of gray, concrete buildings, is a few hundred yards away. It is home to 2,700 people. Many of the apartments have been vandalized and the windows boarded up. Rats scamper around the rubbish chutes late at night. Soldiers long ago put out the lights in some passageways to thwart snipers. Drunk men urinate in the dark stairwells.

Male unemployment is 22 percent for Ulster as a whole, and in Catholic ghettos like Divis Flats, the figure is twice that. According to a recent survey, 7 out of 10 heads of household are jobless. Alcoholism is rampant and child abuse is increasing. Fathers often don't know how to cope with their errant sons. "Sometimes they go overboard and beat them badly," says Colette Davison, a Belfast school psychologist, "and then they get scared and back away." Some fathers are taken off to prison, and the young boys start to act up when they are left alone with their mothers. By the time the fathers reappear, the psychologist says, the children have become teen-agers, and by then it is too late.

According to Frank Shiels, who runs a youth club in the flats, "The sense of morality has crumbled. People have virtually no drive. They take the easy way out—thieving or watching while it's done. If your friend steals somethings and sells it to a fence, then there are a few drinks in it for you."

Sean Nolan says he has tried getting work as a motor mechanic, but has been turned down. "When they hear you're from Divis Flats," he says, "when they hear you're a Catholic, you're hammered." He has spent little time in school over the years, but he doubts that makes much difference. "I know a whole lot of lads with good educations," he says, "and they still can't get jobs."

And so Sean joined the ranks of the hoods. They range in age from 14 to 25. A few of the older ones try armed robbery, but most go in for breaking into homes, warehouses, cars and shops. They don't indulge in the muggings and rapes so typical of many urban ghettos; women can walk the streets of Belfast without fear at all hours of the night, even in areas where the police have not dared to walk for years. It is the local shopkeeper, no longer able to get insurance, who suffers most from the hoods; one liquor store has been hit 53 times, and the proprietor ruefully suggests that he might apply to the Guinness Book of World Records.

"Invariably," says Shiels, "they get caught. Virtually every kid I work with, and I could name 70 to 80 off the top of my head, is up in court. A lot are facing long sentences. But their attitude toward life is, 'Here today, no concept of tomorrow.' It shows in everything.

"They do the most stupid things. One tried to steal the lead from the roof of the Queen Street police barracks. It wasn't that he set out to get the barracks as some sort of political act or anything like that. Kids had been stealing the lead from all the buildings up to it, and the police station was just the next in line."

Sean Nolan doesn't watch much television, but he says his favorite program is "Starsky and Hutch." He explains: "I like the way the two try to be good cops, but they're con men as well." There's one thing he doesn't like about them, though. "They never get shot dead. They're like Tom and Jerry—all kinds of things happen to that cat, but you never see that cat gettin' killed. That's what I like about John Wayne. I've seem him get killed."

One real killing that stands out in Sean's memory happened when he was 10 years old: Four British soldiers on a routine patrol in Divis Flats were blown up in a stairwell. "Their legs were lyin' here and there," he recalls. "One was squashed against the wee railing. I felt sorry for them soldiers. Everybody felt sorry for them; a whole lot of people were crying. But they shouldn't join the army if they know things like that's gonna happen." Today the site is called the Crying Stairs. "People has seen things on them," Sean says. "Spirits or something like that. They feel different from other stairs, far different."

For the hoods, violence and danger have a special attraction. They steal cars, not for profit, but simply to relieve their boredom, and they drive the cars through army checkpoints without stopping. The soldiers, afraid that the vehicle bearing down on them contains a terrorist out to kill them, sometimes shoot at the occupants. Ten people have died in such joy rides in the last 18 months, some from bullet wounds, some in accidents. Many more have been seriously hurt.

"I think death and injury is a normal thing," says the Reverend Matt Wallace, who serves a parish in West Belfast. "It is not a significant event in their lives." When a proposal to involve joy riders in a stock-car racing program was put forth last year, one Catholic bureaucrat said he didn't think the race track would provide enough excitement. "I think you'll have to have someone shooting at them as well," he said.

Sean reflects that view. "You spot a car and you want to steal it," he says. "If a car is good enough, you can't resist." And that goes even for someone who has been shot at. "It was a good lot of shots—machine-gun fire," Sean recalls. "When you see them pointin' a gun, you be scared, but when you hear the gun, you're not afraid. It's all over in five seconds." Many of his friends have been less fortunate: "We hanged about with half them ones that was shot dead. Paul Moan—'Big Hippo' his nickname was—he was shot dead. We used to hang about with him. Another wee lad, Chico—Seamus Magill we hanged about with him. He was shot in the shoulder; now he has a wee hump in the shoulder. You know Egger? He was shot in the lung. He got the last rites twice. Georgina Maguiness was shot dead. A wee girl like she was."

According to police reports, 1,850 cars were stolen in West Belfast last year. Sean says there may be 100 car thieves from Divis alone. He learned the technique—he says he can steal any car with a single key and a penknife—at age 15. Often, he says, he and his mates stole six or seven cars in a single night. They traded in slow cars if they saw a parked one that looked faster. When they ran out of petrol, they just lifted another car. If there was something of value in the car, so much the better; they could sell it down in the flats. They stole cars that belonged to policemen and cars that belongs to IRA members. They stole cars out of parking lots near the city center and out of the driveways of houses. The only cars that were relatively exempt were Raleigh sports cars, the RS 2,000, painted white. "Those cars are unlucky," says one of Sean's pals. "A wee lad and a girl were shot in one. Once I had one and I knocked a woman down."

Adult responses to the joy riding—as to the hoods in general—have been varied. Community leaders in West Belfast have denounced the shooting of teen-agers as "summary execution," too severe a punishment for car theft. The police have tried to ram the stolen cars with armored Land Rovers and arrest the occupants, but the Land Rovers are cumbersome and slow. The joy riders often elude them and head for Divis Flats, where they are home free. They know the police don't dare leave their vehicles to give chase on foot for fear of being ambushed.

By bringing the stolen vehicles into the flats, the hoods enter the bailiwick of another armed authority, the Provisional IRA. The Provos, as they are called, don't care whether the hoods steal cars; they do care about actions that bring the police nosing about in West Belfast. Yet, night after night, despite being threatened with the traditional IRA punishment of being shot in the knee, the hoods whizzed around the district. If death didn't stop them, why should a mere kneecapping?

Jim (Gangster) Devlin, 18, was shot in both knees and both elbows on June 8. A Provo spokesman explained: "Gangster Devlin was shot for activities that included armed robbery, hijacking cars, breaking and entering, and beating people. No one I know in Andersonstown [a West Belfast district] shed one tear when he was done."

Sean Nolan remembers "another wee lad" he used to hang about with who was shot in both elbows and both knees. "The only thing that's wrong with him now," says Sean, "is he's very thin, because he was shot that many times. He wasn't just shot for stealin' cars, he was shot for other things as well, but he still stole cars after that, so he did. He was a wild one. See, if I got shot, I wouldn't steal cars again."

According to police, there were 834 kneecappings in Ulster between 1973 and 1980. Most of them took place in Belfast, and roughly three-quarters of them were done by Republicans, the rest by the Protestant paramilitaries, the Ulster Defense Association. It is a private matter: Catholics shoot Catholics, Protestants shoot Protestants. Some police authorities believe that the frequency of kneecappings in West Belfast varies with the attitude of the community toward the IRA; when the acceptance of the Provos is high, the people have a greater tendency to bring their complaints to the organization to mete out punishment.

According to Richard McCauley, press officer of the Provisional Sinn Fein, the IRA's political wing, there are firm rules governing kneecapping. "No one is kneecapped who is below the age of 16," he says. "If he is under 16, he might get a beating. I'm not talking about breaking his arms or legs, but a beating is a beating." Before any one is kneecapped, the press officer says, he is given a series of warnings.

McCauley says that most people are actually shot not in the knee but in the thigh. "They're in the hospital for a day or two," he says, "and they hobble around for a week after. It's more the scare that's effective than the injury itself. It's awfully frightening to sit and watch a man pointing a gun at your leg. You have to be very bad to be shot in the knee, and if you are very, very bad, you are shot in the kneecaps and elbows."

Kneecap victims have little choice but to go back to their neighborhoods, where they are intended to be limping examples for those who would stray from the straight and narrow. In a study conducted six years ago of 86 punishment shootings, Dr. James Nixon, an orthopedic surgeon at Belfast City Hospital, found that amputation occurred in about 10 percent of the cases. He estimates that one in five kneecap victims will walk with a limp for the rest of his life.

"It always crosses your mind when you see a young man on crutches," says Father Wallace of West Belfast. "He may have a football injury or some other problem, but you always wonder what he's been kneecapped for."

Eamon Kelly (not his real name) is a 25-year-old hood, the older brother of one of Sean's mates. Accused of theft, he was offered the choice of being kneecapped or cleaning the walkways in Divis Flats. Cleaning sidewalks was a humiliating prospect, he says, and so he chose to be shot. Eamon received compensation of $7,400 under a British Government program that provides payments for terrorist-connected injuries. Many hoods, knowing that Belfast's hospitals are world-famous for their expertise in these repairs, see a clean, no-complications kneecapping as money in the bank.

For Eamon, there were complications. The damage to his leg was considerable, and the government confiscated half of the grant to pay what he owed in back rent and utilities. He says he and his pals drank the remaining $3,700 in six weeks. Eamon mentions that he was punished for theft even though many IRA families were buying the stolen goods from him and even though his brother had recently done time in the Maze Prison for the movement, but he supports the Provisionals, nonetheless. "Put it this way," he says. "They must have thought I needed it to keep me in line. And when you get a guy who starves himself to death, my kneecapping is nothing compared to that."

Sean Nolan says he once escaped a kneecapping only after his father pleaded for mercy. An IRA man, whom Sean describes as "very polite," released the teen-ager with the promise that if Mr. Nolan didn't look after his son, the next time around both of them would be shot. Yet Sean says he doesn't fear the Provos. "Are you afraid of the American Army?" he asks. "They're your own people, aren't they? Well, I'm not afraid of the IRA."

Nor does Sean see much wrong with kneecapping. He even wishes it on some hoods he thinks have gone too far. "The ones I would like to see kneecapped is the young ones," he says, "because them wee ones is picking up car thieving and they can't even see over the steering wheel. They're stealing cars and running them into a wall for pure badness. They're giving us a bad name."

Some hoods hate the Provos and are quick to point out that, while the IRA defends its own right to steal cars and rob people, hoods are kneecapped for doing the same things. Clergymen and politicians also denounce the Provos whenever a young man is kneecapped. And even some IRA members disapprove of the practice, but, lacking their own prison facilities, they claim they have no alternative—and some form of crime control must be exercised.

Says the Sinn Fein's McCauley: "We're talking about thousands of kids. In Divis Flats, you're talking about 9-year olds. I've seen them sitting on the balconies absolutely drunk. You can bring them to their families and talk to their parents about it, but you're often talking about a family with six or seven children in a two-bedroom flat. Inevitably there is conflict between the parents, partly because they can't make ends meet. Despair is the only thing they really know, and the will to control their kids is just not there. What do you do?

"The way these hoods see it, if you were kneecapped, that's something to be proud of, and if it's been done twice, that's better. They're looked up to by other hoods. It's not a very happy state of affairs because we are not dealing effectively with the problem. But you've got to do something. Our people demand that we do something."

In the other Belfast, Protestant paramilitary groups face similar demands. But while Catholics go to the Provos because they don't like or trust the Royal Ulster Constabulary, Protestants go to Andy Tyrie, head of the Ulster Defense Association, because they believe his group is sometimes more effective than the R.U.C. "A lot of times," Tyrie says, "the police can do nothing because the situation is too complicated or because they can't get the guy to sign a statement admitting he committed the crime."

Kneecappings are far less frequent in East Belfast. Tyrie inclines to give the Protestant hoods "the same punishment they gave someone else. Say they beat up somebody, the same might happen to them. For a very serious offense, say a rape or if they really beat somebody badly, they might be kneecapped." Like his IRA counterparts, Tyrie professes not to like the job. "This is not a normal society," he says. "You have to instill fear in those sorts of people, but it never works if it occurs over a long period of time."

There are similarities between the hoods of the two Belfasts. They have taken to glue sniffing in about equal numbers. The truancy rates are comparable. The Protestant lads might have a little better chance of getting a job, but not by much. (The shipbuilding industry, for example, which once employed 25,000, now supports fewer than 7,000 jobs.) And hatred of the police is hardly limited to Divis Flats. The legend "SS-RUC" is scrawled on walls in Protestant areas, and the police admit that, when they go out to maintain order at soccer matches between Protestant and Catholic teams, they suffer far more abuse from the Protestant mob.

The difference between the hoods of East and West Belfast is more clearly seen in the kinds of crime they commit. The Protestant hoods don't go much beyond burglary and theft; according to Alan Darnbrook, a senior probation officer, they may have a worst record in this regard than their Catholic counterparts. But the hoods of West Belfast are singular in their devotion to danger—stealing cars, hijacking and burning trucks, rioting.

The third force of law-and-order in Belfast, the Royal Ulster Constabulary, has nothing but criticism for its irregular competitors. "Kneecappings," says a police spokesman, "originate in kangaroo courts." Yet many Protestants and Catholics who would agree with that judgment also find the constabulary's version of justice unacceptable. They point to charges of brutality during interrogation procedures, charges made by the Police Surgeons Association and by Amnesty International. Indications are that any physical mistreatment has now largely stopped, yet controversy continues over police practices under various special laws enacted to deal with terrorism.

In Northern Ireland it is legal, under these measures, to arrest someone and hold him for a week without ever charging him with a crime. A government tribunal has reported that two-thirds of those arrested under the emergency legislation during one 12-month period were never charged with any crime. The R.U.C.'s Chief Inspector, Herbert Norris, comments: "On the night of a bombing, we might arrest 30 people and bring them in for questioning. Twenty of them might be released and 10 of them charged. Two-thirds seems to me a reasonable figure."

Moreover, the legislation requires that those arrested by the police must have some connection, at least as witnesses, to a terrorist offense. But in a recent survey conducted in association with the London-based National Council for Civil Liberties, two-thirds of a group of 48 people arrested under the measures in the preceding six months said they had never been asked about any specific incident. They said they'd been asked, instead, about their families, about their political views and the views of their neighbors, and about where they drank and with whom. Dermot Walsh, who conducted the survey, has concluded that the R.U.C. never had any intention of charging these people, that its chief objective was to build up a dossier on those arrested and their neighbors. Inspector Norris denies such charges. "The police," he says, "have more important things to do."

More than a third of those in the council survey said the security forces had tried to enlist them as informers. Some said they were offered money, others that they had been threatened. A teenager claimed he was told that soldiers would approach him as he stood in his local pub with his friends and that the soldiers would say, "Are these the lads you were telling us about?"

These arrests, called screenings, usually occur at 6 A.M., and are made by police in bulletproof jackets, sometimes backed up by army units. Some people have been arrested repeatedly, presumably to keep their files up to date. A Protestant whom Walsh interviewed said he had been arrested 27 times and held for a week on several occasions, yet had never been charged.

Sean Nolan says that he has been arrested seven times, always at 6 A.M., and that he spent occasional nights in prison along the way. In the flats, such incidents are so common that they are hardly remarked upon the following day. Provisional spokesmen and community leaders claim that once arrested, some hoods have agreed to provide information about the Provisionals in exchange for freedom from prosecution. "If the kid agrees to be an informer, the police protect him and pay him," says the Reverend Desmond Wilson, a West Belfast priest paid by the city council to work as a community organizer. "For the IRA," Father Wilson says, "every young fellow brought in for a crime is a possible informer, so it is in their interest to control crime."

On June 17, the R.U.C. picked up Vincent Robinson, 29, a father of two, from his Andersonstown home. Nine days later he was shot through the head by the IRA. His body was found in a rubbish chute in Divis Flats. The IRA claimed that Robinson had agreed to give the police information on local Republican activists, and that he was being paid $11 per day for his services. "We would remind the public that, if arrested and taken to Castlereagh or any of the other interrogation centers, the R.U.C. will attempt to recruit them as informers," said the IRA's statement on the killing. "We would also remind the public of the inevitable and very serious consequences for anyone who agrees to cooperate with the enemy."

The Provos have very strong views on all behavior that has political implications, and hoods like Sean ignore them at their peril. It is permissible, he says, to steal from stores within the security cordon that surrounds Belfast's center—but stealing in Castle Street, a street just outside the security barriers that is patronized almost entirely by Catholics, will land you in big trouble.

Similarly, only certain kinds of hijacking are countenanced. The hoods hijack a vehicle by pretending to have a gun or by waving bricks menacingly at the driver while blocking the path of the truck. If the vehicle is commandeered in order to station it across a road as a barricade during a riot, says Sean, no Provo will complain. The problem arises with any suspicion that you are hijacking for profit.

"You can't steal anything off them," Sean explains. "You can't drive it around. Say you stole a big lorry full of bikes—you have to burn it all. The Rah [the IRA] would shoot you for looting. They want to show that the lorries are not being stole out of greed."

Sean is not convinced of the wisdom of this policy. "See some of those lorries," he says, "the owners make money. Say a bus comes up here and you hijack it. Think of the money that's on the bus, all the money people paid to ride it. The driver will say you hijacked the money as well, and he'll keep it for himself. There's plenty of people that have gotten claims who put their own lorries in the middle of the road. He says, 'You can burn that one there,' and he walks away, and he tells the cops, 'They hijacked my lorry.' See, everybody is making money except for the ones that is doin' all the hijacking."

Given the limited police presence in West Belfast and other Catholic ghettos and the difficulty of separating terrorist crime from what the army calls "ordinary decent crime," the dimensions of the crime wave in Northern Ireland are hard to assess. But the increase clearly has been enormous. Between 1969 and 1980, for example, the number of offenses reported to the police rose 230 percent and the prison population quadrupled. According to the government, there are some 2,500 people now in prison, 220 of them in young-offender centers. Northern Ireland, which 13 years ago had the lowest prison population per capita in Western Europe, now has the highest.

Larry Murtagh, a welfare worker in West Belfast, offers the explanation of what those figures mean: "Nearly every house we go into has someone inside one of the prisons, and their week may be geared to getting on the mini-bus and going for the visit. Years ago, I'd go into these houses and they'd have just a picture of the Sacred Heart hanging on the wall. Now the place is covered with plaques and homemade crafts made in prison. When you walk in and see them, you know immediately that there's someone inside."

According to recent government figures, two-thirds of those now serving long-term prison sentences in Northern Ireland were under the age of 15 in 1969 when the troubles broke out; one-third of them were under 9. The hoods of West Belfast recognize that they may also be in line to spend large chunks of their lives in a prison cell. They're willing to take the risk.

Psychologists say that a chief reason for emotional disturbance in children is a sense of not belonging, of not fitting into their community. The children who have grown up throwing stones in riots, facing the common foe in the shape of a soldier or a policeman, belong. They may have given up regular church attendance, a major break with tradition in this very religious land, limiting themselves to attending funerals. They may have made aggression, in the words of the psychiatrist Morris Fraser, their "major means of dealing with all problems." But in the opinion of some authorities, they have found a way to deal with their world that produces a minimum of mental illness—considerably less, for example, than in many of the ghettos of the United States.

Those parents whose children have not yet become hoods devise their own strategies. "Yes, I am keeping him at home," one mother told a school psychologist who was investigating her son's truancy. "I know where he is when he is at home. He is not with the IRA, he is not hijacking cars, he is not playing in derelict buildings. He is watching TV, and I have a fire, and he is warm."

The daughter of the house is not really part of the drama. The sexes keep to their traditional roles in Northern Ireland: Women have the entire responsibility of raising a family. No man ever does the laundry, makes the dinner or goes to the grocery. Men drink, gamble, steal, go off to jail, or get involved in paramilitary groups. The wives are left behind to cope.

What the visitor to Northern Ireland finds most amazing is that very capacity to cope. Tony Spencer, a member of the Belfast school board and professor of sociology at Queen's University, puts it this way:

"Everyone has adapted very well. There are certain areas people will not go into, certain things they will not do, but that is no different from the United States. The paramilitaries have adapted. The security forces have adapted—the death rate is far higher in Germany on the autobahn, and the training the troops get here is excellent. The fire service has adapted: We have people from all over the world coming to look at it to see how it works. Medicine has adapted: We have doctors coming from all over to study the way we deal with high-velocity gunshot wounds. Public administration has been strained, but it has adapted, and you haven't seen anything approaching the breakdown you saw in Italy during the earthquake, for example. The political system goes on, after a fashion. Unemployment is bad, but lower than in Latin American states. The milk keeps arriving in the morning. The bread is in the shops every day. We can go on like this indefinitely, for generations."

Sean Nolan, however, is ready for change. About three months ago, after the death of another joy rider and the capture of many of his pals, he decided to go straight. Of course, he helped in the rioting after the deaths of the hunger strikers, and he took part in hijacking a few vehicles at the time, but other than that, he says he's stolen hardly anything at all. He doesn't particularly like this new way of life, but he thinks he'd like jail less. "Since I stopped stealin' cars, it's really boring," he says. One of his brothers works in a Belfast factory, and Sean thinks he may get a job there sooner or later.

For he is dreaming about getting married and having 15 kids. "With these troubles," he says, "you need plenty of big sons to back you up." He'd like to raise the family in Andersonstown. "My sister lives there. It's very quiet, clean, spotless like. Around here it's paint bombs everywhere. As long as my family would be away from this here." Sean pauses. "Then," he resumes, in a more familiar mode, "I could just travel down here for the action."

REPORTER AT LARGE[3]

. . .There is a traditional Ulster song called "The Old Orange Flute,"which—like many traditional things in Northern Ireland—casts a long light on Matthew and Marie's situation.

The song tells of a young Protestant weaver, Bob Williamson, "a stout Orange blade," who played the flute in the Twelfth of July parade, which each year celebrates William III's victory over James II at the Battle of the Boyne. In retentive Irish memories, this battle is renowned for preserving the union of Ireland with England under Protestant kings. However, Bob Williamson proves not so stout after all. He marries "a papish called Bridget McGinn" and turns papish himself. When the local lads get upset about his treachery, he has to flee across the county border with his wife and possessions. His old Orange flute loyally goes on playing the Protestant repertoire—"Croppies Lie Down," "Kick the Pope," and "The Boyne Water"—and, though—finally burned as a heretic by a council of priests, plays to the last:

> While the flames roared around it
> They heard a great noise,
> 'Twas the old flute still whistling
> "The Protestant Boys."

The song manifests some of the elements that give Northern Ireland its character: a widespread belief that historical events are of contemporary importance; a general intransigence, often taking the form of stubborn patriotism; and a common inability to treat any subject as purely secular. Much energy is expended by scholars and pundits on whether the evident division in Northern Ireland is basically religious, political, or cultural. It appears that in fact all sorts of accumulated old differences are maintained and enlarged for reasons of social distinction and self-esteem, and are used by both politicians and clerics when they want to enlist their

[3] Excerpt from article entitled "Reporter at Large: Matthew and Marie," by Anthony Bailey. *The New Yorker*. p 51-61. My. 8, '78. Copyright © 1978 by Anthony Bailey. Reprinted from *Acts of Union: Reports on Ireland, 1973-1979*, by Anthony Bailey, by permission of Random House, Inc. Originally appeared in *The New Yorker*.

supporters; then the labels Nationalist and Loyalist, Catholic and Protestant are handed out, and people wear these labels proudly.

It would be difficult to prove that people in Northern Ireland are more religious than people elsewhere. It is known that they go to church more than most people in Western Europe: something like nine out of ten Catholics in Northern Ireland attend Sunday Mass; more than five out of ten Protestants are believed to go to church on Sundays. Belfast appears to have more church buildings than similar-sized cities: steeples still create much of the city skyline; at sidewalk level, church notice boards are conspicuous. One Belfast cinema was converted not long ago into a church. Although many Protestant ministers complain about Catholic Church interference in politics in the Irish Republic, Northern Ireland is remarkable for the number of Protestant clerics who are politicians. One of the best known is the Reverend Dr. Ian Paisley, M.P., whose strident Calvinist voice can be heard from the pulpit of the Free Presbyterian Church on Ravenhill Road, which is reckoned to be—apart from the cathedrals of Liverpool and Coventry—the most expensive ecclesiastical structure built in the United Kingdom since the Second World War. Many periodicals have obvious religious affiliations—Paisley publishes one called the *Protestant Telegraph* —and religious bookshops are common. Indeed, in a city where clerical collars and "Repent Ye Must" sandwich boards are a frequent sight, local people find nothing exceptional in religious graffiti, such as a slogan painted on a wall off University Road: "SAM TODD FOR GOD." Todd is a star player for the Linfield soccer team, whose supporters are Protestant, and whoever scrawled this message was presumably drawing attention to the close link that Linfield supporters believe exists between the Almighty and His team.

If one splits open the vicious circle of interlocked problems in Northern Ireland—which is something that the printed word allows one to do, though in daily life the circle is a vortex, whirling mercilessly—one can see that a large segment of it is education segregated on religious lines. A few play groups have attracted both Protestant and Catholic infants. A few state grammar schools have a small number of Catholic students. But problems arise from these minglings, beyond bullying and name-calling. Catholic children attending state schools have been refused confirmation by their bishops. Some Catholic students in state schools are told by their parents not to mention the fact that they go to Mass on Sundays. A proposal for an experimental mixed school was effectively blocked by a Catholic bishop's refusal to allow a Catholic chaplain to give religious instruction to Catholic children who might attend it. A group called All Children Together, which is working for unsegregated education in Ulster, was refused permission to use a Catholic church hall for a meeting. It is, by and large, the Catholic Church that insists on separate education, and in many cases the Catholic clergy are prepared to back up the insistence with threats to Catholic parents of hellfire and purgatory; but undoubtedly the segregation has the support of many Protestant ministers and teachers. One young Catholic woman who taught for a while in a Belfast state school did so under an assumed name and without telling her colleagues she was Catholic. After she left and the truth came out, there was a great uproar; several teachers said they would have objected to her presence among them if they had known.

The system tends to perpetuate two somewhat archaic visions of citizenry and loyalty. Teachers go to training colleges run by the state or by the Catholic Church, and intellectual border-crossing is not encouraged. Catholic schools teach the Irish language and promote a nationalist Irish allegiance. Protestant schools exalt the binding tie with Britain. Both visions obscure the fact that Catholics in Northern Ireland have not voted with their feet to move to Southern Ireland (where economic opportunities and social benefits are fewer), and that Ulster Protestants also feel a very strong attachment to their country—they are at once Irish *and* British. Although the Gaelic natives of Ireland (the descendants of aboriginal Irish and of Celtic invaders) have been infiltrated by Vikings, Normans, Scots, and English over a good twelve hundred years, and some Anglo-Irish families date their arrival in Ireland to the twelfth century, roughly a century after the Norman conquest of England, the popular view in Northern Ireland is that anyone from the British Isles to the east is an invader—particularly those people who came from Scotland, full of the fire of the Reformation, in the seventeenth century. The fact is, though, that some of the Scots—including many of Gaelic descent—who settled in Ulster before the Mayflower reached America were Catholic. Cromwell, infamous in Ireland, was equally ruthless to Scotch Presbyterians and Irish Catholics, and he also expelled all Anglican clergymen from their Irish parishes in order to install his own men. Protestant Ulstermen have led political campaigns for Irish independence. Protestant Irish of English ancestry fomented rebellions in the South against British rule.

Yet the simplified view of history has its effect, and, whatever the lines that have been crossed in the past, undermining generalizations, there is no doubt that the lines are now distinct, and often take the form of barricades. Intermarriage between English and Irish was possible before the Reformation. With those who have arrived since, particularly those from Scotland (despite their own Gaelic ancestry), little mixing has occurred; the two tribes have grown apart. There are Catholic names, like Seamus Murphy and Sean Flanagan, and Protestant names, like Ian Forsythe and David Simmons. Dunne with an "e" is Catholic, without it Protestant. (Anthony Trollope entitled a book "The Kellys and the O'Kellys.") The segregation has gone on for so long it has become genetic. Or, at any rate, Ulster people can recognize Catholic features and Protestant features: differences in shape of eye, height of checkbone, color of hair. Sandy hair like Matthew Ferguson's is Protestant, carroty red is Catholic. Protestant men have a confident swagger, Catholic men a lighter, jauntier step. Catholics are smaller. Protestants have conspicuous shoulders. In Belfast, moreover, the locals can, with a Henry Higgins-like precision, relate accent to home address within a street or two, and that enables them to tell which side someone belongs to. To an outsider, both Catholics and Protestants seem to speak in a mixed Irish-Scottish voice, its modulations having more to do with education and occupation than with religion; all use, whatever their class or income, "whenever" for "when," and constantly apply the diminutive "wee"—for example, "Here's your wee receipt," or "Don't forget your wee umbrella." ("Wee" seems to have little to do with size. A shipowner collecting his new three-hundred-thousand-ton vessel from Harland & Wolff's shipyard might well be told, "Here's your wee tanker.") Each side has nicknames for the other: Catholics are Micks, Taigs, or Fenians; Protestants are, curtly, Prods or Blacks. They start to use these as children, after school, when they encounter children from the other side; sometimes, of course, the children from the two sides feel bound to fight. Since they hardly know one another, each side has persistent misconceptions about the other: to Protestants, all Catholics have twelve children and live in squalor; to Catholics, all Protestants behave like participants in a drunken football crowd. Each side has its own signs and symbols (the Harp of Erin; King Billy on a white horse), its own exhortations ("Up the IRA"; "To Hell with the Pope"), and its own days for parading and celebrating.

The Protestant drums beating during the July 12th parade, commemorating King William's victory at the Boyne, arouse in Catholics apprehension and old grievances, dating from a long period of Protestant domination of Ulster life. This domination resulted in the gerrymandering of political constituencies and in discrimination in employment and public housing—all designed, Catholics felt, to keep them an inferior caste. The gradual elimination of these abuses—as the Northern Ireland government was prodded into reforms by the civil-rights movement of the late nineteen-sixties, by some of its liberal-minded supporters, and by an anxious British government in Westminster—persuaded many working-class Protestants that they were losing their edge. They were encouraged in this view by the sermons of their ministers and by editorials in papers like the *Protestant Telegraph*. Papism was on the march—the Pope would soon be running Belfast shipyard—and they were going to be dragged into a united Ireland, where *they* would be the minority. They don't like what they see or hear of the South: divorce prohibited under the Irish constitution; contraception illegal; Catholic bishops attempting to block government health schemes; beggars in the streets of Dublin. Northern Protestants are convinced that the Catholic Church is trying to beat them by weight of numbers. Indeed, one priest, Father Denis Faul, of Dungannon, a town east of Belfast, has publicly suggested that Catholics keep up a high marriage and birth rate precisely in order to outbreed Protestants, and has thereby enhanced Protestant fears—even to the point, it appears to some, of "justifying" the assassination of individual Catholics by Protestant psychopaths or gunmen, who tell themselves they are reducing the chances of a Catholic majority. (Catholics average four births per family in Northern Ireland, Protestants three per family. But more Catholics quit the country, mostly for England, because of limited opportunity, and so far the ratio between the two sides has stayed roughly the same.)

Protestant fears are also intensified by what has happened to the Protestant population in the South: it was three hundred and forty-three thousand in 1901 and a hundred and forty-four thousand in 1961, and is estimated to have been declining at ten percent per decade since then. The Southern Protestant is a member of a dying species. There are various reasons for this, but undoubtedly one factor is that about a quarter of the Southern Protestants marry Catholics and most allow their children to be brought up as Catholics: Bob Williamson's "treachery" goes on. Thus, although the Catholic Church officially disapproves of mixed marriage—to such an extent that priests have been known to declare that a Catholic woman is better off marrying a drunkard than a Protestant—Protestants feel that mixed marriages are one more Roman weapon in the long battle to overthrow the Protestant ascendancy. They believe that the Catholic Church's position on mixed marriages is one of implicit superiority: Bob is expected to be converted, or "turn," or, at any rate, allow his children to be Catholic. This makes for great bitterness. Most mixed marriages appear to involve Protestant men and Catholic women, perhaps because Catholic women strike Protestant men as more submissive or a better homemakers. Some of these marriages result in conversions, but most, it is felt, simply in the husband's going along with what, as a result of her upbringing, his Catholic wife more decidedly wants. And consequently many Protestants feel all the more strongly opposed to mixed marriage. Even if they didn't have a strong Calvinist predisposition to abhor Rome and condemn any sort of union with it, Catholic success in this respect would give them cause to do so. A recent Presbyterian Church statement on mixed marriage said, "Greater problems arise where the man or woman is a member of some special sect or of the Roman Catholic Church." Presbyterian ministers have refused to take part in joint marriage services with Catholic priests. Anyone who steps outside the lines is a traitor. In 1968, a leading Protestant politician, Phelim O'Neill, M.P., was expelled from the Orange Order—a form of Protestant religious and political brotherhood—for attending a community service in a Catholic church two years before.

No official figures are kept of the number of mixed marriage in Northern Ireland. From records kept by one Catholic and two Church of Ireland dioceses, it seems that more mixed marriages are taking place in Catholic churches than before. However, it also seems that in the last few years fewer of all marriages occurring in Northern Ireland have been mixed. (In the rural Catholic diocese of Armagh, which spans the border between Northern Ireland and the Republic, three percent of the marriages taking place in Catholic churches in 1974 were mixed. In Belfast, the figure for mixed marriages taking place in all church and registry offices may be ten percent.) Although nearly everyone in Northern Ireland knows of a mixed marriage somewhere in his own family, it is assumed that fewer mixed marriages are occurring than before the Troubles, particularly among working-class people, because of the hardening of ghetto frontiers and the greater dangers involved. Even among middle-class and well-educated young people, it has become more difficult to make contact across the religious divide. At Queen's University, the students are split roughly fifty-fifty, Catholic and Protestant, and, for the most part, have throughly nonsectarian ambitions and anxieties—to do with their studies in quantum mechanics, say, or the novels of D. H. Lawrence. But students have noticed that co-religionists now seem more inclined to band together; they tend to sit with their own side in the libraries or in the students-union dining room. These are undergraduates who have been in primary and secondary school through the years of renewed Troubles since 1969.

Yet Queen's is still common ground, where boy and girl may meet with less of the tribal impediment hanging over them, and, despite a bomb or two in University Road and several murders last year resulting from an IRA campaign against businessmen with offices in the area, the university neighborhood, with its cafés, pubs, cinemas, and theatres, is safer than many other parts of the city—though restaurant-goers still favor the tables at the back, away from windows, which may in a terrible instant become splinters of flying glass. The indications and effects of violence are ever present: headlines of assassination and terrorism; patrolling Land-Rovers manned by flak-jacketed soldiers, weapons at the ready; loose paving stones—in ill-repaired sidewalks outside bombed buildings—that tip under pedestrians and eject a stream of accumulated rainwater. Yet Belfast, at least for its middle class and its students, remains a city with two good newspapers, a serious fortnightly magazine, a thriving theatrical and artistic life, an excellent annual arts festival. New buildings rise; hotels are repaired, bombed, repaired again. One hears fewer sirens than in New York. There are fewer murders proportionally than in Detroit. There are more fatalities from traffic accidents than from terrorism. But violence has perhaps not been reduced (as a previous British Home Secretary hoped) to "an acceptable level." It appears to be organic; one will have to produce different people in Northern Ireland in order to do away with it.

For people who are in a sense different already—who, it is evident, are not easily lumped with one side or the other—the risks are clearly considerable. Their existence is a rebuke to the fanatics in each camp. The dangers are more constant in working-class areas; on some streets no mixed couple would now dare to live. Many who were born and brought up in such districts have cleared out to England upon marrying someone from the other side. One couple who ran into difficulties are the Millars—to give them the pseudonym that was used for them in a study on intimidation done for the Northern Ireland Community Relations Commission in 1973. Mr. Millar was a Protestant, Mrs. Millar a Catholic, and they lived for eleven years in a public-housing development a few miles north of the city. Then, in mid-1971, trouble began. Some of their neighbors were involved in sectarian disputes, but the Millars were subjected to abuse and intimidation from both sides. Their car tires were slashed; their house windows were broken; obscenities were painted on their walls and footpath; they were cursed and threatened. They abandoned their home and moved in with relatives, but were soon forced by further threats of physical violence to move on. Since a safe area for Mrs. Millar was a dangerous one for her husband, the family split up: the children stayed with their mother, and their father got a room of his own in a Protestant area. However, they were fortunate enough to be able to get a mortgage and buy a house on a private estate farther outside the city, where they are now living together again.

Similar cases are known. One mixed family moved four times because of intimidation, and the husband, a Catholic who worked on building sites where most of the laborers were Protestant, eventually became so frightened that he took his family to England. One mixed couple were petrol-bombed out of their house on the Shankill Road and machine-gunned in the Falls Road house they next moved into. Following that, the man was badly cut up in what he believes was an attempt to murder him. Some mixed couples have tried to defend their property—by putting barbed wire in the garden, for instance—but most feel that such actions would merely advertise their predicament. Some never answer the door at night. The ring of the telephone can be terrifying: a threatening caller, whose name you don't know, knows who *you* are, where your wife works, and where your children go to school. And, of course, moving isn't always a complete escape. One working-class Protestant who is married to a Catholic woman now drives a taxi on the Falls Road. In the eyes of those he has left, he has turned, like Bob Williamson. His children go to a Catholic school, and although he is secure among Catholics, and is doing well (taxis tend to run on sectarian routes, crowded with passengers, and are highly profitable), he is trapped in the Falls Road area, terrified to leave it. One Shankill man, whose family had run a grocery store in the Shankill Road for twenty years, had to move out when he married a Catholic. He moved to Stranmillis, an improving middle-class district, but even there he and his wife have been subjected to snide looks and nasty gossip, and they continue to worry about what else might happen.

For behind the looks and the words is always the chance of death. Again, no figures exist for the number of mixed couples who have been murdered, but there have been several tragic cases. The methods used on occasion remind one of the savage practices of the Gauls—of punishments meted out in the Germanic forests to those threatening the solidarity of the tribe. On September 2, 1972, a Protestant propaganda sheet called *Loyalist News* asked,

"What prominent member of the SDLP"—an almost entirely Catholic political party—"is keeping company with a Protestant female from Belfast's Crumlin Road?" The following June, the SDLP man, Senator Paddy Wilson, and his friend, Irene Andrews, were found stabbed to death. Senator Wilson was firmly opposed to violence and, unlike most Ulster politicians, did not carry a gun; his body had thirty knife wounds. Responsibility for this deed was claimed by a group of Protestant "paramilitaries" calling themselves the Ulster Freedom Fighters. One twenty-year-old Protestant girl (who talked some time ago to the Canadian journalist Kevin Doyle) had been married for roughly twelve hours to a young Catholic laborer when she became a widow. Her husband was abducted from their flat in the Shankill Road area. His body was found in a country ditch a few days later. He had been castrated, tortured, and murdered with a shotgun blast to the back of the head. . . .

IV. WHAT NEXT?

EDITOR'S INTRODUCTION

In the years between 1618 and 1648, a general war was fought in Europe that became known as the Thirty Years' War. Although religion was not the sole issue in the war, it was one of the prime causes, setting Protestant and Catholic states one against the other. It is no wonder that Constantine FitzGibbon, in the first selection in this book, refers to the Troubles as a continuation of that war. If his analysis is correct, what conceivable solution could there be after all these centuries? At present, there seems to be no clear answer to the question even though attempts are constantly being made to find one.

In the first selection, by Trevor Beeson in *Christian Century,* the author reviews the problem and finds that some form of unification is inevitable—but not just yet. Countering this view in the second selection, Jack Beatty, writing in *The New Republic,* believes that a remedy for the Troubles in Ulster would be for the Catholic minority to have a full political role in the government. He maintains that religious differences would fade and that, in accordance with history and the will of the majority, Northern Ireland should remain an integral part of Britain. In the next selection, William Borders, writing in the *New York Times,* reports that the British government intends to abide by the wishes of a majority of the voters in Northern Ireland. Mr. Borders, citing trends, points out that Catholics are increasing at a considerably faster rate than Protestants, suggesting that the solution to the problems may simply be a matter of time.

In the fourth article, another *Times* report by Mr. Borders, he notes that increased economic cooperation between the governments of Great Britain and the Republic of Ireland might help in resolving conflicts. He also describes a meeting between the Prime Ministers of both countries that could forge ties that would ultimately result in some form of amity. The meeting, following a Republican bomb attack in London, was denounced by Unionist leader, Ian Paisley, who resents England's direct dealings with the Republic. Paisley's arguments against unification and for union with Britain follow in an excerpt from a letter in the *Washington Post*. He makes a plea for Ulster's right to be British. A fundamentalist minister and politician, the Reverend Mr. Paisley presides over that segment of the Unionist forces whose more extreme elements have adopted terrorist tactics that can be compared to those of the IRA.

In the sixth selection, Terrance G. Carroll, writing in *Political Quarterly,* applies the theories of conflict regulation of the Irish situation and recommends that the only solution that seems to fit the problem is a form of mutual veto—by Unionists and Catholics alike—over policy decisions, and he insists that only the British government is in any position to impose such a solution.

In the final piece, John Hume, Leader of the Social Democratic and Labor Party from Londonderry in Northern Ireland, and one of the most respected and successful mediators in the country today, argues in *Foreign Affairs* that negotiation and a mutual respect for compromise on both sides are absolute requirements, if a way out of the impasse is to be found. He maintains that unification would be in Northern Ireland's best interests, if it is achieved in a peaceful manner.

NORTHERN IRELAND'S ORDEAL[1]

The deaths of Irish Republican Army hunger strikers Bobby Sands, Francis Hughes and Raymond McCreesh—and now Patrick O'Hara of the Irish National Liberation Army, an IRA offshoot—may not be the last in a series of suicides in Northern Ireland's Maze Prison. Other prisoners are refusing food, and if and when they die their places will be taken by some of their comrades, nominated by the IRA leadership. The moves are dramatic,

[1] From article entitled "Northern Ireland's Ordeal: No Easy Solution," by Trevor Beeson. *Christian Century.* 98:629-30. Je. 3-10, '81. Reprinted by permission. Copyright 1981 Christian Century Foundation.

macabre, and certain to arouse a great deal of public concern—
which is the main aim of the exercise. They also create a good deal
of confusion among those who are not well acquainted with the
Irish situation, and this again is useful to the rebel cause of the
IRA and such splinter groups as the INLA.

Britain's Problem

Although nothing in Ireland is ever quite as simple at it
sounds, a few facts are beyond dispute. For historic, cultural and
religious reasons, accumulating over a period of 300 years, Ireland
is now divided. The greater part of this fairly small island constitutes the independent Irish Republic (Eire), with its still largely
rural life and staunchly Catholic culture. The northeast corner of
the island (Northern Ireland) is a province of the United Kingdom. Here the great majority of the population are
Protestants—the descendants of settlers from Scotland and other
parts of Britain in the 17th and 18th centuries—though there is
a substantial Catholic minority, some of whom have their roots in
the area; others were attracted from the south by the prospect of
work in the growing industrial towns.

From a geographical and economic point of view, the case for
a united Ireland is overwhelming. It is also fair to say that it would
be no great loss to Britain if Northern Ireland were to be detached
from the United Kingdom and taken into the Irish Republic. The
people of the Republic want this to happen; so do the Catholic minority in the north. But the Protestant majority in the north are
determined to remain within the United Kingdom and would, if
necessary, fight to prevent their absorption into a united Ireland
where they would form a religious and cultural minority.

Hence the current problem facing the United Kingdom. Over
the years Britain's handling of Irish affairs has been deplorable
and indefensible, and the present crisis is undoubtedly due to serious mistakes in the past. But past mistakes are not always easy
to correct, and Britain's post-World War II politicians, who were
not involved in any way in Ireland's past, have been faced with
a seemingly intractable problem. Simply to abandon Northern
Ireland would be undemocratic, inasmuch as it would be against

the expressed wishes of the majority of the people in that province. It would almost certainly lead to a civil war in Ireland. On the other hand, the case for a united Ireland cannot lightly be dismissed, and the terrorist activities of the IRA over the past decade (designed to drive the British out of the north) have seriously dislocated the life of the province, cost more than 2,000 lives, and required a military presence in areas where the Catholic minority is strong and militant. The British government is in a no-win situation.

IRA Prison Demands

This is the broad background of the Maze Prison hunger strike. The prison itself is a modern one and used for convicted terrorists—mainly members of the military wing of the IRA, but including also a few Protestants who have taken violent action against Catholics in reprisal for IRA bombings and shootings. The hunger strikers are not, it is important to note, concerned with more humane prison conditions. The regime in Maze Prison is more liberal than in most other prisons in western Europe. The demand for civilian clothing and so on is concerned with changing the status of the terrorists so that they will be regarded as political prisoners rather than as criminals. They also wish to run their own compounds, with their own leadership, discipline and punishments—on the lines of a prisoner-of-war camp. They see themselves as soldiers in a war of liberation, not as ordinary criminals.

The British government is prepared to concede none of this. In a province where fully democratic procedures exist, and where military activity is confined to the containing of violence, the justification for a "war of liberation" seems much less than in, say, one of the Latin American dictatorships. Indeed, to the Protestants of Northern Ireland the activities of the IRA are those of a minority seeking to coerce a majority. It is true that this majority constitutes some sort of occupying force, inasmuch as its origins were alien, but after 300 years of occupation the Protestants regard themselves as every bit as Irish as their Catholic adversaries. The British government also points out that, whatever the motives of the

IRA, the men in Maze Prison have been convicted of serious offenses against innocent people—the maiming and killing of men, women and children who, apart from their presence in the province, where they have spent the whole of their lives, can in no sense be regarded as an occupation force. When hunger striker Bobby Sands died, it was noted by many politicians and church leaders that his death was the result of his own free choice; his many victims were given no such choice.

Need for Reconciliation

Granted all this, however, it is sometimes argued that the British government would be wise to make most if not all of the concessions demanded by the Maze prisoners, if only to lower the temperature on the streets outside. Hunger strikes have a long and honorable history among Irish republicans, those who die in this way are regarded as martyrs, and a death of this sort inflames passions, with the result that violence increases and the overall problem becomes even more difficult to solve. This is an attractive argument, not least to Christian commentators who believe that reconciliation requires acts of generosity and sacrifice. But it seems only too plain that if the Maze prisoners were granted what amounted to political status, the ranks of the military wing of the IRA would swell dramatically overnight. The fact that its present members receive long prison sentences if convicted of terrorism deters the less valiant brethren from active involvement in the IRA, and the fact that they are treated as criminals, rather than as prisoners of war, places a question mark over the nature of the struggle. Any encouragement of the IRA would therefore lead to more violence and make the task of reconciliation even more difficult.

This is how the British government sees things, and the issue is one of the very few on which all the main political parties in Britain are agreed. In this they have the support of the main British churches, which are naturally pained and embarrassed by the religious element in the Irish conflict but recognize that there is no easy solution to any of Ireland's current problems. Does the lack of easy solutions mean, however, that there is no solution short of a bloody war in which the strongest wins and takes all?

In the short term, the answer is probably yes. There seems not the faintest prospect of Northern Ireland's Protestants severing their links with the rest of the United Kingdom. Equally, the IRA seems determined to continue with its policy of violence. Skilled police and military action is therefore essential if peace and order of some sort are to be maintained. In the long term, Ireland will be united—perhaps with some form of federal government, and with ample protection for minorities. But this is still a long way off. Considerable changes will have to take place in the outlook of the people, and in the social structures, of both north and south before there can be much movement toward political unity. The Protestant and Catholic churches, which remain strong, have a crucial part to play in bringing about these changes—though it would be quite unrealistic to expect quick miracles. Meanwhile, the violence which fuels antagonism must be contained, and it should be recognized both in Ireland and in other parts of the world that the IRA terrorist, far from being a hero, is an enemy of the best interests of all the Irish people.

THE TROUBLES TODAY[2]

. . .Irish history extends back to the time of the fabulous personages who stud Yeats's early poetry with unpronounceable names, but the part of it that still shapes the present is the long, painful interval of British rule. Another Irish Protestant writer, Jonathan Swift, wrote a parable which catches the essence of this rule as well as the self-deceit by which the British long were able to look upon brazen plunder as a humanitarian act. Every year, the parables goes, the British would dispatch good men to govern Ireland; but every year, halfway across the Irish Sea, pirates would board their ships and replace them with brigands, who would then land in Ireland and do unspeakable things in the name of the Crown. Undaunted, His Majesty's government would send

[2] Excerpt from an article by Jack Beatty, literary editor. *New Republic.* 183:17-21. N. 15, '80. Reprinted by permission of *The New Republic,* © 1980 by The New Republic, Inc.

out more good men the next year and the next, but still the pirates would come. They have been coming for 800 years.

An Elizabethan apologist for the genocidal campaign then being conducted against the Irish wrote that "they live like beasts, voide of lawe and all good order"; they were "more uncivill, more uncleanly, more barbarous and more brutish in their customs and demeanures, than in any other part of the world that is known." There was only one thing to do with such people and that was to replace them with loyal settlers. In 1609 the English King James proclaimed a land settlement for Ulster in which four-fifths of the six counties were set aside for the exclusive occupancy of English and Scottish settlers; the native Irish were either driven out or forced to live in reservations which they could not leave on pain of death. This is how the Irish province of Ulster came to have a Protestant majority living in anxious domination over an unreconciled Catholic minority. This is how the Troubles began.

From 1609 to the present the story changes, but it always has the same three sides: the English, the native Catholic Irish, and the settler population made up of English and Scotch Methodists and Presbyterians. After the partition of Ireland in 1922, the British recede, leaving Ulster to be governed in its domestic affairs by a parliament which brazen gerrymandering makes into a Protestant club. That leaves the Catholics and the settler Protestants. To this day, they are taught different versions of the past in schools that remain segregated by religion. For the Catholic children, the great days of history are the Catholic days, while for the Protestant children the day of days is July 12, 1690, the day when the good Protestant king, William of Orange, defeated the bad Catholic king, James II, at the Battle of the Boyne, thereby ensuring that Ireland would remain under British rule for the next 250 years. In Northern Ireland, history as it is preserved in memory is a means not of social unity but of social division. Since, moreover, the state supports the Catholic schools as well as the public schools attended by the Protestants, it is not too much to say that, next to welfare, Northern Ireland's chief social investment is prejudice.

A Protestant children's rhyme:

Sleuter, slaughter, holy water
Harry the papishes every one
Drive them under and bate them asunder
The Protestant boys will carry the drum.

A Catholic children's rhyme:

On Saint Patrick's day, jolly and gay
We'll kick every Protestant out of the way
And if that won't do we'll cut them in two
And then send them to hell with their red, white and blue.

Protestants say they can spot a Catholic by the color of his eyes, or by his hair—red being an infallible sign of Catholicism. Names also help. Riley is a Protestant name, for example, but O'Reilly marks a Catholic. Each side, writes Anthony Bailey in his excellent *Acts of Union* (Random House), has nicknames for the other. "Catholics are Micks or Taigs. Protestants are, curtly, Prods or Blacks. They start to use these as children, after school, when they encounter children from the other side; sometimes of course the two sides feel bound to fight."

Marriage might bridge the gulf, but in fact intermarriage itself is, in the words of one expert, "probably the single biggest divisive issue in Irish life." The former bishop of a Protestant diocese in the North wrote in last month's *Encounter* that "the pressing problem which faces all Christians in the North is the problem of their relations to their fellow Christians; the problem not only of coexisting peaceably with each other, but of how to prevent inherited beliefs and attitudes from coming into collision." The title of the bishop's article sums up what I have been saying in five words: "It is a religious issue!"

In the face of such deep divisions, it is easy to see why men and women of good will fasten on the substitute issue of H Block. It is wholly in the present; it does not stretch back to King Billy and King James. It is equally easy to see why even a temperate man like Anthony Bailey can give way to the gloomy verdict that "the violence appears to be organic; one will have to produce different people in Northern Ireland in order to do away with it." Fantasy or despair: the visitor to Ireland meets with these polar attitudes again and again.

From the Dublin government there is the fantasy of the "Anglo-Irish dimension." This, they say, will bring an end to the Troubles by putting the queen on the Irish coinage, permitting contraception, and making divorce as common as daisies. These steps taken, the Ulster Protestants will break the connection with England and merge with the Republic of Ireland in a veritable *frisson* of fellowship which will make them forget their primordial fear that to live in a Catholic-dominated state is to let themselves in for Kipling's "Hells Prepared by Rome." From the able political men of the Social Democratic and Labour party, which represents the province's 500,000 Catholics, there is the same Republican fantasy: any internal settlement in the North must look toward union with the South. This stipulation, of course, destroys the chance of an internal settlement, since the Protestants will not agree to share power with Catholic politicians pledged to abolish the present state. From the Sinn Fein, which is the front organization of the IRA, there is the fantasy of a socialistic Ireland which will spring into being as soon as the last British soldier is gone. To prepare for this millennium the Ulster Protestant must, as a Sinn Fein spokesman put it, "be educated." "By bomb?" I asked. "By bomb, if necessary," he answered.

The other side is no more realistic. From the Democratic Unionist party, which orchestrates the grievances of Ulster's 1.5 million Protestants, and which boasts its most popular politician in that redoubtable cleric, Ian Paisley, there is the neo-colonial fantasy of continuing to rule in Ulster without sharing power with the Catholics. As for the British, they make a show of enthusiasm for their new power-sharing plan, but they have been ruling Ulster since 1972, and underneath one suspects that, like the Dublin man I met in Dingle, they wish "the whole bloody place would float out to sea."

The British now are hot for a political solution, but their soldiers—8,000, down from 20,000 seven years ago—are accoutered in flack jackets and armed as if for the D-Day landings, and the only hearts and minds one can imagine them winning would have to belong to members of the National Rifle Association. There have been just under 1,500 civilian deaths during what the British call "the Emergency," and one has to wonder how many of these people were killed by promiscuous firing from soldiers armed with automatic rifles. Nor is it any better with the police. The Royal Ulster Constabulary carry submachine guns with long clips of ammo which probably could be squeezed off in seconds, causing God knows what carnage in the ricochet. The armament—and I have said nothing of the tanks sitting by the country roads or the armored cars and personnel carriers which are as common in Belfast as Volvos in Georgetown—must seem excessive to any visitor. It chills the air. It confronts you with the insensate mechanism of state violence which vastly exceeds the violence of the terrorists in destructive power, if not in deliberate cruelty. And it is brutalizing and intimidating. In the short time I was in Belfast the sights of the guns made me nauseous, faint; made me know the coward in myself and, against my prejudices, left me with a sneaking respect for the IRA.

Politically, it is stupid for the British to display all this weaponry, for it galls the Catholics, whom it is clearly meant to intimidate, while it stiffens the will of the Protestant ultras, who would rather die than compromise. Blunder, bluff, and force—these are old British habits in Ireland, and it is hard to make the case that Britain has changed when five armored cars may go by you in 15 minutes in the center of Belfast. In dealing with the Troubles as a military problem, the British have made the province ungovernable. They have reason to despair.

My idea of the Troubles was formed in the early 1970s by Marcel Ophuls's documentary, *A Sense of loss*. Its most striking feature is mob violence—sectarian warfare between working-class Protestants and Catholics. This violence is augmented and confused by the presence of the British troops. When they were first called out of their barracks in the summer of 1969, they were seen as the protectors of the Catholic minority, its traditional protector, the IRA, having faded away. (In those days, beneath the "IRA" scrawled on Belfast and Derry walls was written "I Ran Away.") But since Bloody Sunday, January 30, 1972, when British paratroopers shot 13 Catholic demonstrators in Derry, the British (at any rate in our picture of them) have become the scourge of the Catholics, breaking into their homes, shipping them off to internment camps, and driving their young men into the arms of the resurgent IRA. Just about here our picture of the Troubles freezes. Few of us remember the prorogation of the Stormont parliament in 1972 and the advent of direct rule from London. Fewer still retain any memory of the several truces, abortive settlements, and failed governments since then. It has been eight years.

Today Northern Ireland is a far less dangerous place than it was eight years ago. In August 1972, for example, there were 460 reported shootings and 136 bombings, whereas in June of this year, the last month for which statistics are available, the figures are 38 and 14. Mobs no longer bash it out in the streets. The violence is now almost exclusively of a military nature. It is the work of the IRA terrorists. Their violence provokes the answering violence of the Protestant terrorists, the police, and the Army.

The steady decline in violence is full of political meaning, and what it chiefly means is that the IRA has lost much of its support in the Catholic ghettos. To use the Maoist analogy, the sea in which these fish hide is receding, leaving them exposed and isolated. Increasingly desperate, the IRA now terrorizes the very people it claims to protect. One measure of this: since the first of the year, there have been 58 IRA kneecappings. The victims: Catholics. It is the way the IRA deals with potential witnesses. There are also reports of flourishing IRA protection rackets in Belfast and Derry. It is as if the IRA is devouring its own political base. Why? Apparently the American Irish are beginning to see through the IRA propaganda, and the money from America is drying up. Gangsterism is the shortrun solution. It could spell long-run disaster.

The British estimate that fewer than 300 terrorists are active in the whole of Ireland; and now a new factor, the Irish Republic, is cracking down on them. It will not be their haven any longer. IRA suspects are routinely tried in British courts with evidence furnished by the Irish police. So, North and South, it has become more dangerous for the terrorists.

The bitterest denunciation of the IRA I heard—"Fascist thugs"—came from a civil servant high in the Dublin government. This man spoke with moral authority, since his father had belonged to the original IRA in the days when it won Ireland's independence. The Provos, he said, with their PLO-supplied weapons, were a disgrace to this proud tradition. On the other hand, I talked to a Dublin man who maintained that the Provos were in fact upholding the tradition. He spoke of them as "the boys," and made jesuitical excuses for the boys who had just killed two Irish policemen. This man asked "If it was right for the IRA to do what it did in 1919 to 1922, then why was it wrong for doing the same thing in 1980? In the 60 years between, the aim has not changed a bit—to get the British off this island!" He was fiery and articulate, so I feared saying to him then what I say now: that the six counties of Ulster are indeed part of the Irish nation, but belong to England because that is the wish of a majority of their people. By contrast, in 1919 a majority of the people in the South were for independence from England. The 1919 IRA therefore had a democratic basis, whereas the 1980 Provisional IRA is antidemocratic. Terror, not the will of the people, is its God. It is trying to coerce the Protestant majority into changing its mind about the connection with England. It has no chance of succeeding, nor has it any chance of bullying the British into pulling out. Ulster will remain a province in the United Kingdom.

In its propaganda the IRA says that its enemy is the British. It is an effective way to appeal to a venerable moral simplicity among people of Irish blood that England is the source of all their country's political evils; but the reality is of course much more complicated, politically and morally. To paraphrase Conor Cruise O'Brien, contemporary England is not responsible for the troubles of contemporary Ireland, though the record of historical England is damnably black in this regard. To contemporary Britain, Ulster is an expensive international embarrassment. It would love to sever all connections with the province and be rid of the Irish question forever, but in a ripe irony the Ulster Protestants will not let if off the hook of its own history. In political as opposed to propaganda terms, then, it is the Ulster Protestants who are the real enemy of the IRA. It is important to understand something of the way in which the Irish past has shaped the character of these people, for otherwise it is too easy to write off their moral aims.

In a nation where memory is the major form of mind, the Ulster Protestant is distinguished by his bottomless sewers of historical recall. History is a nightmare from which he never wakes. The

Irish historian F.S.L. Lyons has defined the psychology of the Ul-
sterian as a "siege mentality," and has traced its provenance to the
Siege of Derry in 1689, when that Protestant army put up a heroic
defense against the assault of the Catholic army of King James
I. A Catholic army, this time the IRA, was at the gates again when
the present Ulster state was born in 1922, and in the 60 years
since, the pressure from that quarter has never wholly waned.

Fearful of the threat from the South, fearful too of the restive
Catholic minority—breeding, breeding—within its gates, the Ulster Protestant also lives in warranted fear of being abandoned by
his British protectors. Twice in the last century Britain was ready
to pull out, and on both occasions the Ulstermen were ready to
fight to maintain the Union. In 1885 they were prepared to take
up arms against Gladstone's Home Rule bill. They had formed
a massive secret army to fight in 1914 when Home Rule again
seemed imminent, and were checked just this side of treason only
by the outbreak of World War I. And some knowledgeable observers think that if Britain were to pull out of Northern Ireland today, the Ulstermen would engage in a desperate guerrilla war
against both the Catholics and the departing British troops.

To grasp why the Ulster Protestants are so impassioned about
the Union with England, it isn't necessary to go as far back as the
Siege of Derry. It is enough to drive across the border from County Monaghan in the South of Ireland to County Fermanagh in the
North and look at the monuments in the town squares commemorating the Ulstermen who have died in all of Britain's modern
wars, from the Crimean to the Boer, from the Great War to the
war of 1939-45. It was a regiment of Ulstermen that was the first
out of the trenches on that horrific opening day of the Somme in
1916, and July 1 is still a day of national mourning in Northern
Ireland. The monument outside the Queens University of Belfast
is thick with the names of members of the university community
who died in places like Tobruk and Burma. While the Republic
of Ireland, in a gesture of anti-British neutrality, sat out World
War II, Ulster guarded Britain's northern flank, and destroyers
based in Belfast and Londonderry and Larne sailed out to meet
the convoys from America, preserving Britain's lifeline. It was an
inestimable service, and for it Churchill paid Ulster a tribute

which any English MP tired of Ulster's high welfare payments should read as a text on the nature of historical obligation:

We were alone and had to face single-handed the full fury of the German attack, raining down death and destruction on our cities and, still more deadly, seeking to strangle our life by cutting off the entry to our ports of the ships which brought us food and the weapons we so sorely needed. Only one great channel remained open. That channel remained open because loyal Ulster gave us the full use of the Northern Irish ports and waters, and this ensured the free working of the Clyde and the Mersey.

Ulster's loyalty cost it some 5,000 casualties, among them many civilians killed in two punishing air raids on Belfast. But Ulstermen have died in thousands for the British flag whenever Britain needed them; and it is this blood sacrifice which gives their descendants a claim on Britain she may ignore only at the price of dishonor. Finally, therefore, the IRA is up against what all those monuments in that little country stand for: a connection with England that has been sealed in blood and witnessed in repeated acts of loyalty. It constitutes a kind of moral gravity, and this is a far stronger force in history than the legalisms and the economics by which shallow intellectuals set such store.

Britain should bear the drain on its treasury and the loss of its sons and stand by Ulster as Ulster once stood by her. But this does not mean that it would be morally indelicate of the British to put pressure on the Protestant politicians to work with their Catholic opposite numbers in setting up a devolved government. The Ulster Protestants have grown used to a position of uncontested domination. But power cannot obscure reality forever, and the Protestants now are faced with a choice. If they want to play the leading role in any devolved government, they will have to accept the full participation of the Catholics in every sphere of its operation. Otherwise, the British will continue the present system of direct rule. It will be hard to give up the old dream of a "Protestant Parliament in a Protestant country," but it is that or nothing for the Reverend Paisley and his followers.

But the Catholics of Ulster also will have to give up a dream. A political settlement is only the first step toward softening the enmities between the Catholic and Protestant working classes, but even it never will be taken unless the Catholics accept the fact that they are an Irish nation in the British state. In other words, they will have to abandon their dreams of uniting with the Irish Republic. As so often in Ulster politics, memory can only be an irritant on this score. For as any Catholic will tell you, the partition of Ireland was intended to be temporary. The border, which meanders through pastures and living rooms all the way from Newry to Donegal, was an expedient the British hit upon to extricate themselves from a nasty guerrilla war in the South without triggering another in the North. The idea was that they would gradually pressure the Ulster Protestants into becoming part of the fledgling Irish Free State. This, at any rate, is what Lloyd George on the one side and Michael Collins on the other envisaged would happen when they signed their names to the Anglo-Irish treaty of 1922. That it did not happen was a great tragedy for the whole Irish people. It was a tragedy for the Protestants because, from 1922 to 1972, it allowed them to exercise a morally dangerous degree of power. This proud people became the masters of a state founded on bigotry, discrimination, and fear. It was a tragedy for the Catholics because it left them stranded in a country in which they were regarded as a kind of fifth column for practicing the faith of their fathers.

But there, a short distance to the south, was the Republic of Ireland, the land of milk and honey and Protestants who knew their place. For 50 years, whenever a Northern Catholic suffered an indignity at the hand of a Protestant, he could retreat into his paradisal fantasy. Then in the mid-1960s, history played a cruel trick on Northern Catholics. For a brief moment it seemed as if their prayers might be answered as the two states of Ireland began to draw closer together. At home, an indigenous civil rights movement, inspired by the black freedom marchers in America, was winning concessions from the Stormont government—in the shape of fair housing legislation, equal opportunity guarantees, and one man-one vote redistricting—unimaginable only a generation before. Pope John XXIII was extending an ecumenical hand to Protestantism, and after centuries of doctrinal antagonisms, Catholics and Protestants were rediscovering their common heritage in the body of Christ. But even the hopes raised by Pope John paled beside the well-nigh eschatological expectations roused by the 1965 meeting, in Northern Ireland, of the prime ministers of the two states of Ireland, Sean Lemass of the Republic and Captain Terrence O'Neil of Ulster. This unprecedented event must have seemed a portent to the Northern Catholics. If the leaders of the sundered states could meet, could real union be far behind?

Then it all went smash. Hope rapidly turned to fear as Captain O'Neil's concessions stirred the dormant Protestant working classes into a belated frenzy of reaction. Long excluded from political participation by the club of Anglican squires who had run the country since 1922, the Protestant masses now mobilized behind the defiant rhetoric of Ian Paisley. The first and unhappiest result of this upsurge was the collapse of Captain O'Neil's reform government and its replacement by a ministry less willing to meet the ever growing demands of the Catholics. It was only a question of time before Catholic demonstrators should clash with Protestant counter-demonstrators in the narrow streets of Belfast and Derry.

In retrospect it seems clear that the unpredictable element in this fated chain of events was the recrudescence of the IRA. By the late 1960s the IRA was hardly an army at all; after an earlier terror campaign in the 1950s had failed to win Catholic support, the IRA renounced direct action and adopted instead a Marxist line which called for the peaceful means of indoctrination and education to achieve the unvarying Republican goal. The outbreak of street fighting between mobs of Protestants and Catholics in 1968 caught the IRA unawares. Faced now with a choice either to continue in its seminar phase or to resort to direct action, the organization split into wings favoring both extremes.

Divided, the IRA might have been paralyzed altogether had it not been for the infusion of some £75,000 to the wing favoring the use of force, the so-called Provisionals. This money, which was quickly used to buy weapons, came from the Dublin government under circumstances that remain as mysterious as they are scandalous. For here was a government that had fought the terrorists on its own soil giving them the means to ply their terrorism on the soil of a neighboring country. When the present Dublin government denounces as fascists the terrorists who now kill their policemen, Northern Protestants should not be accused of undue cynicism if they doubt the sincerity with which these denunciations are made. For the current prime minister of the Republic, Charles Haughey, was, the minister of finance in 1969, the very man who approved the clandestine transfer of funds of the Provisional IRA. To be sure, the Dublin government acted under the impulsion of a not unjustified fear that the Catholic minority in the North was about to be destroyed by angry Protestant mobs. No doubt the Dublin government intended that the IRA would act exclusively in its traditional role as the guardian of the Catholic ghettos. They could not have foreseen that the appearance of British troops (called out of their barracks, ironically, to do what the Dublin government hoped the Provos would do—protect the beleaguered Catholics), just weeks before the £75,000 was delivered, would give the Provos the chance to go on the offensive and to widen a virtual civil war into an anti-colonial guerrilla war.

What has since happened in the North is that the Provisional IRA has succeeded in putting the issue of breaking the connection with England on the agenda of the Northern Catholic politicians. But what do the Catholic people think? Professor Lyons reports that a poll taken in the late 1960s, before the pot of the Troubles had boiled over, indicated that, while a majority of Catholics were in favor of unification with the South, it was not an issue of great importance to them. It was not then a cause in Ulster politics. The Catholic civil rights groups were demanding equality *within* the British state of Northen Ireland, not the ending of partition. Doubtless feeling among them is very different today. After all, they have been living these past 10 years in what the IRA is pleased to call "a war zone." They have their own siege mentality; in bad times, the Irish Republic is their England, and these past 10 years have been very bad times indeed. But surely it is not beyond the wisdom of the leading Catholic politicians to recognize that a large part of the Republican feeling among their constituents is in the decisive instance a wish for peace and safety and social hope for their children. Peace, security, a normal, happy childhood for their children, equal opportunity and equal rights for themselves—can't the Catholics have these things within a reformed Northern state?

What might such a state look like? Above everything, it would have to be a state the Catholics could respect and in whose political life they could participate. In these features, it would bear little resemblance to the colonial regime that lasted from 1922 to 1972, though it might be the state that Ulster was in the process of becoming when the Protestant reaction and the rise of the IRA plunged it into anarchy. It is certain that this reformed state could not escape from the politics of religion, and for a time Catholics and Protestants would vote as opposing blocs, threatening the state with political paralysis. But it is possible to imagine even this fixed feature of Ulster politics changing under the assault of political ambition. For the 30 percent Catholic minority would loom irresistible to any Protestant politician who wished to challenge the hegemony of Reverend Paisley, the real toad who inevitably would be the first prime minister in the imaginary Ulster garden. A coalition of Protestants and Catholics—a party, say, of the professional and middle classes—might topple Paisley and his party, and perhaps even govern as a coalition. Posit such a situation and it becomes easier to imagine the Catholics coming to identify with the state of Northern Ireland. The troubles have shown that the old state cannot work, not that *no* state can work. Politics can deepen social rifts, but it can heal them too.

The fantasy is perhaps no more credible than the others. But it does differ from them in one respect: it is not a *total* fantasy. It preserves a daunting dose of reality in the shape of Ian Paisley. It preserves the connection with England which, as we have seen, the Ulster Protestant will not suffer to be broken so long as his memory is green. Unlike the die-hard Protestant fantasy, however, it includes the Catholic minority as full political actors, while it puts the Republican dream of the Catholics on the back burner of history, where it belongs. Finally, this legitimate polity I am positing is one in which terrorism has no social soil in which to grow. I assume that the IRA will outrage itself out of business. The IRA had to abandon its earlier terror campaign for lack of support among the Catholics, and many observers think the same thing is happening now. Still, there is one incalculable difference between the early 1960s and now: with the backing of the Terror International based in Libya and South Yemen, terrorism can now survive without an indigenous social base. That the outrage of a purely parasitic terrorism will further polarize the two communities is the gravest threat confronting any reformed state. It will take international action of a concededly unlikely kind—boycotts, quarantines, the ostracizing of the PLO and the minions of Colonel Qaddafi—to contain it. If the United States has any role to play in bringing social peace to Ulster, it lies in leading an international offensive against terrorism.

Aside from this last implausibility, this scenario has roots in social actuality if not yet in any social movement. The immense war weariness in Northen Ireland is making for it. The desire of a religious people to wring meaning from the years of their collective life that will always be known as the Troubles is making for it. The ambition of political men tired of being ruled from London is making for it. The fact that the present British government does not depend for its majority on the votes of Ulster MPs makes for it. The growing evidence of realism about the IRA among the American Irish is making for it. Against these positives must be ranged the negatives of the international recession, which has hit Ireland hard, compounding the social poisons of prejudice with the insecurities that flow from heightened economic competition; and the free market sink-or-swim theology of the Thatcher government, which soon may find sinful the subsidies necessary to get Ulster's promising enterprises—an automobile plant, for example—off the ground. Then, too, there remain the obdurately colonial mentality and manner of the Ulster Protestants which are not likely to change overnight. There remains the equivocal position of the Irish Republic which on the one hand condemns the terrorists and on the other lends legitimacy to their cause by espousing the same political line: that the connection with England must be broken. But the greatest negative in the current situation is presented by the Catholic politicians of the North, who continue irresponsibly to dangle the dream of joining the Irish Republic before their frightened constituents. It is up to them to break the grip of Ulster's history on its politics by reconciling their people to the necessities of their situation as a minority in a democracy split along religious lines. Until the day when the politics of religion gives way to the politics of class or coalition, the Catholics will lack the social weight of the Protestants. This will be true even in a reformed state. No one can deny that such a disparity will be felt as a deprivation.

The political realm is the sphere of existence in which men can transcend the fate of their history. To enter this realm is to accept the possibility that something new might happen. By refusing to enter it, the Catholic politicians are ensuring that the cycle of futility will continue. They look to the past for security and the past enfolds them like a doom. In Ian Paisley, Ulster has a great demogogue; but what it needs now is a Catholic statesman to transform the desire for peace among his people into the strength necessary to renounce a dream and reclaim an imperfect reality. The moment is ripe; it awaits the man.

ULSTER SEEMS HEADED FOR A CATHOLIC MAJORITY[3]

Residential neighborhoods in this troubled province tend to be segregated along religious lines, and the visitor can often tell, just by looking around, which side he is on.

One clue is the Union Jack, which flies only in Protestant neighborhoods. Another is whether the graffiti that can be seen everywhere are directed against the Pope or against Queen Elizabeth II.

Yet another clue is the children. There are usually many more of them on the streets of a Roman Catholic neighborhood, because the Catholics tend to have bigger families. On that demographic fact of life here rest political implications of enormous significance.

The Catholics are still in the minority in Northern Ireland, but their proportion of the population is growing. Many Protestants regard the steady increase in the Roman Catholic population as a demographic time bomb.

[3] Newspaper article by William Borders, reporter. *New York Times.* Mr. 14, '82. © 1982 by the New York Times Company. Reprinted by permission.

"Inevitably, there will be a Catholic majority in the north within my lifetime," said a Protestant college student here, adding that "people my age better begin to adjust to the idea."

Successive British leaders have pledged that this province will remain British for a long as its majority wished. But if most of those who could vote were Catholic, it would presumably choose union with the Irish republic.

For various reasons relating to the sectarian violence, statistics on religion and population are inexact in Northern Ireland. But it is thought that in 1978, for the first time, more children were born to Catholic parents than to Protestants. There were 26,239 births that year, and the Roman Catholic Church recorded 13,286 baptisms.

According to Paul Compton, a professor of geography at Queen's University here and a student of the population trends, the birth rate among Catholics is 21 per thousand, as against 14 per thousand for Protestants. Because the Catholic population has become progressively younger, its death rate is considerably lower than that of Protestants—9 per thousand as against 13 per thousand.

Mr. Compton estimates that Catholics made up 38 percent of the population in 1979. But no one knows for sure, and the results of the 1981 census appear likely to shed little light on the matter.

Not only is the question about religion voluntary, with many people refusing to answer it, but the whole census, like so much in Northern Ireland, is charged with sectarian politics as well.

Some militant Catholic nationalists who refuse to recognize the sovereignty of the British here boycotted last year's census for political reasons, as they boycott elections conducted by what they regard as an illegal government.

In the census, a door-to-door canvasser in a Roman Catholic neighborhood of Londonderry was stopped on the street and shot dead. That halted the census there and discouraged other census takers from being overly thorough in similar neighborhoods.

Another unknown factor is emigration from the province. Usually, more Catholics than Protestants have left. But "the troubles," as the last 12 years are generally called, have produced dissatisfaction and fear in a previously complacent Protestant population.

Although the Protestants, the side that wants Northern Ireland to remain British, still constitute a majority, Prime Minister Margaret Thatcher tacitly acknowledged for the first time last November that it was possible that the majority here might change.

In a joint communiqué with the Prime Minister of Ireland, she reiterated the "guarantee" of British rule here for as long as the people wished it. Then the communique added that if the people of Northern Ireland ever voted in favor of changing the constitutional status of this province, "the British Government would of course accept their decision and would support legislation in the British Parliament to give effect to it."

LEADERS OF BRITAIN AND IRELAND TO FORM PANEL ON CLOSER TIES[4]

The Prime Ministers of Britain and Ireland, in a friendly five-hour meeting here today, agreed to set up a joint "intergovernmental council" to work toward closer links between their two countries.

The precise structure and functions of the council were left vague, probably intentionally, since the whole subject is delicate and emotive in the context of the situation in Northern Ireland.

But in news conferences later, both Prime Minister Margaret Thatcher and Prime Minister Garret FitzGerald made it clear that they envisioned a new degree of closeness between their two Governments, a development that is anathema to many Protestants in the North.

[4] Newspaper article by William Borders, reporter. *New York Times*. Mr. 7, '81. © 1981 by the New York Times Company. Reprinted by permission.

'Patterns of Cooperation'

"We really look forward to the time when these meetings are not so remarked upon as they are at present," Mrs. Thatcher said. "We are talking about patterns of cooperation."

After a round of Irish Republican Army bomb attacks in which three people have died in London in the last month, the meetings were held under particularly heavy guard at the British Prime Minister's official residence at 10 Downing Street.

In their joint communiqué, the two Prime Ministers agreed on the need for "efforts to diminish the divisions between the two sections of the community in Northern Ireland," terminology that aroused immediate indignation in Belfast.

The Protestant hard-liners there, ever fearful of being betrayed by the London Government, take the position that the affairs of Northern Ireland are a wholly internal British matter and none of the Dublin Government's business, and that it is therefore inappropriate for the two Prime Ministers even to be discussing them.

"There are simply no circumstances in which the people of Northern Ireland will either accept or acquiesce in any involvement by the Republic in the affairs of their province," the Reverend Ian Paisley, the leading Protestant militant, said in a statement today. "All Unionists set their faces absolutely against any attempt, covert or otherwise, to take us down the road to a united Ireland."

The joint communiqué reaffirmed the British Government's pledge that Northern Ireland would remain part of Britain as long as the majority in Northern Ireland wished it. But it seemed to break a bit of new ground psychologically with a statement that if a majority there ever voted for dissolution of the link with London, "the British Government would, of course, accept their decision." That was contemplating something that the Unionists like to regard as unthinkable.

The two Prime Ministers were accompanied in their talks by their Cabinet officials responsible for energy and foreign affairs, and their discussion covered cooperation in several areas.

According to their communiqué, the two leaders "agree on the need to intensify economic cooperation between the two countries, and between the two parts of Ireland."

Their basic agreement was phrased this way: "Recognizing the unique character of the relationship between the two countries we have decided to establish an Anglo-Irish Intergovernmental Council through which institutional expression can be given to that relationship between the two Governments."

These new contacts, "to discuss matters of common concern," will take place at various levels within the Governments.

Before the meeting this morning, the Irish Prime Minister went to a London hospital to visit one of the soldiers injured in an IRA explosion here last month. He said he hoped that the British people would regard his visit to the 20-year-old soldier as "an expression of our total abhorrence of violence and our intention to work as closely as possible to eliminate this."

IF YOU HAD GIVEN ME A VISA . . .[5]

The message I wish to present to the American people is a message which by and large they have never fully heard. Indeed by virtue of the orchestrated propaganda of certain Irish Americanas and other IRA sympathizers, this message—the message of Ulster unionism—has been grossly misrepresented as one of bigotry and intolerance and as devoid of reason or logic

In reality however the opposite is true in regard to the case of the Ulster majority. Our case is simple. Northern Ireland, in contrast to the rest of Ireland, has been peopled by those of British extraction and governed as part of the United Kingdon for almost as long as the U.S.A. has had its independence. And above all it should be understood that Northern Ireland remains part of the United Kingdom because that is the undeniable wish of the vast majority of the people of Northern Ireland.

[5] Excerpt from Letter to the Editor, by Ian Paisley, Unionist leader. *Washington Post.* Ja. 8, '82.

We remain British not by compulsion but by choice. It is not British troops that keep us British but the freely expressed will of our people through the ballot box.

When in 1921 the south of Ireland decided to secede from the United Kingdom, the north opted to remain as it was—a full part of the U.K. In exercising that right we were only exercising one of the most fundamental rights of all—the right of self-determination.

It is the refusal of a small Republican minority within Northern Ireland to accept Northern Ireland's right to remain British in accordance with the will of the people, which has, through the IRA, led to the infliction of horrific terrorism upon the people of Northern Ireland in an effort to force them to join in an all-Ireland Republic. What the IRA and Irish Republicanism have failed to achieve through the ballot box they are seeking to obtain through the bullet and the bomb.

The struggle in Northern Ireland therefore is about the defense of democracy against the forces of sheer terror. The people of Northern Ireland ask only to be entitled to decide their own destiny, free from terrorism and external interference.

The refusal by a section of the minority community to accept the state of Northern Ireland contrasts sharply with the constructive and democratic role played by the Protestant minority in the south of Ireland, and this in spite of the near-total eradication of that Protestant minority. Whereas theRoman Catholic population in Northern Ireland has increased significantly since partition, the Protestant minority in the south has been reduced over the same period from 10 percent to less than 4 percent of the population.

There can be no doubt as to how the Ulster people wish to be governed, since no later than May 1981—the last time they went to the polls—parties supporting union with Great Britain received over 70 percent of the vote.

Given the overwhelming determination of the people of Northern Ireland to remain British and the terrorism they have suffered as a consequence, it is little wonder that remarks such as those by [then-Deputy Secretary of State William] . . .Clark [to the effect that American public opinion was heavily in favor of the unification of Ireland] are deeply resented as encouragements to the terrorists and are viewed as an unwarranted attack upon the right of self-determination by the people of Ulster.

REGULATING CONFLICTS: THE CASE OF ULSTER[6]

In March of 1980 the British Government adjourned inter-party talks on the constitution of Northern Ireland which had taken place intermittently during the previous three months. These so-called "all-party" talks were boycotted by the Official Unionist Party which won the largest number of seats in the 1975 Constitutional Convention election, and the three parties which did take part were unable to come to any agreement. For six years British Governments had held fast to the view that no progress was possible until the main political parties of Ulster arrived at some agreement among themselves. Now, however, that position changed. The Prime Minister and the Secretary of State for Northern Ireland publicly declared that if these talks failed Westminster would attempt to develop and implement a proposal of its own. Is this a wise decision? Does a British "initiative" have any chance of success?

The resolution of intense and long-standing conflicts between social groups is a process to be measured in generations, and sometimes in centuries. In the short run the best that one can hope for is that the conflict may be regulated, though not resolved. By this I mean that the basic hostility between the groups continues to exist, but their competition is confined to accepted and largely peaceful means. When dealing with democratic societies one must add the requirement that this be accomplished without extensive governmental repression. Only the most naïve could hope for any quick resolution of the conflict in Northern Ireland, but I believe that there are potentially helpful techniques for regulating that conflict which have not yet been fully explored.

[6] Article by Terrance G. Carroll, member, Politics Department, Brock University, St. Catherines, Canada. *Political Quarterly.* p 451-63. O./D. '80. Reprinted by permission.

The Need for an Initiative

Two sorts of objections have been raised to earlier calls for a British initiative. One is concerned with the source of the initiative, suggesting that any useful proposal must come from within Ulster rather than from London. I shall address this question at the end of this paper. There is a second, more far-reaching argument, however, which holds that no initiative will be helpful, no matter what its source. Richard Rose [of the American Enterprise Institute] examined 13 alternative forms of "immediately practicable governance" for Northern Ireland, for example, and found that each could be argued to be undesirable and unworkable. His sombre conclusion was that: *"The problem is that there is no solution."* After reviewing the recent literature on Ulster, J. Bowyer Bell indicated his concurrence with Rose and suggested that, despite all of the efforts made by individuals and by groups, "there is no peace and doomsday waits at the bottom of the lane."

Neither Bell nor Rose would accept that their realistic but gloomy analyses justify eschewing policy initiatives altogether. Indeed, Rose modified his conclusion that there is no solution by adding: "at least no solution recognizable in those more fortunate parts of the Anglo-American world that are governed with consensus." A great many countries in the world do have a relatively stable civil authority without an underlying popular consensus, however, and while none of the alternatives that Rose examined commanded his enthusiastic support, he pointed out that the anticipated consequences of some schemes were much more attractive (or much less unpalatable) than others.

Other observers of Irish affairs do make the easy jump from a justifiable pessimism to an as yet unjustified despair. They suggest that if an Irish Armageddon is inevitable, any attempt to delay its arrival is wasteful folly. British authors who take this view often urge that the British Army be withdrawn from Ulster. They do so not from the Irish republican position that this would contribute to a solution, but rather on the grounds that since no solution is possible one might as well confine the coming casualties to the people of Ireland. I would argue, on the other hand, that open civil war in Ulster should not be considered unavoidable until all other possibilities have been exhausted. If Armageddon is inevitable there is no need to help it along.

One of the easiest tasks for the fledgling futurologists is to predict the likely course of events in Northern Ireland for the next several years. There are only two scenarios that are at all probable:

1. Direct rule continues indefinitely, with a fluctuating but horrifying level of violence. Periodic lulls in the conflict, based on exhaustion and the hopelessness of victory, alternate with recurring outbreaks of strife based on the fear of defeat.

2. The constantly present potential for open and total civil war is realized in a violent cataclysm unparalleled in Europe since the Second World War.

Both of these scenarios are tragic. But these are simply *probable* outcomes; they are not *inevitable*. The nature of the Ulster conflict is such that one cannot conceive of a lasting peace in the absence of a political settlement, and a political settlement is unlikely to be achieved without a conscious effort by the British authorities. A settlement is unlikely even with the best efforts of the British, of course, but less so. There are situations which could develop in Northern Ireland—given all of the constraints imposed by the realities of the existing circumstances of the province— which would be preferable to these more probable scenarios. The horrifying nature of the likely outcomes of Ulster politics makes it worthwhile to devote considerable effort to encouraging these less likely but more desirable developments.

In recent months the British press has expressed considerable resentment of those North Americans who have been urging that Westminster take some "initiative" on Ulster. I quite agree that substantively empty calls for an initiative are unhelpful. All of us who have some experience of Northern Ireland before the imposition of direct rule know that things can be even worse than they are now. Rash policies are more likely to cause change for the worse than for the better. Nevertheless, there is need for careful and constructive thought about the possibilities for planned change in the Ulster situation, if only because continued drift is so fraught with dangers of its own.

Regulating Conflicts

It may be useful to start by surveying the range of techniques which have been successfully applied in other conflictual situations. Eric Nordlinger [*Conflict Regulation in Divided Societies*] has argued that all such techniques fit within six general categories, and that the application of one or more of these "conflict-regulating practices" is a necessary (but not sufficient) condition for the management of intense conflicts. The six techniques are the stable governing coalition, the principle of proportionality, the mutual veto, purposive depoliticization, compromise and concessions. At least four of the six have been attempted to varying degrees in Ulster in recent years.

The mid-1960s were a period in which there was a serious effort to manage the conflict through the evolution of a compromise. The O'Neill Government actively sought the support of Roman Catholics, and efforts were made to improve relations with the South. A process of reform was initiated which eventually produced nondiscriminatory policies on public housing and employment, a new local government system, and the replacement of previously gerrymandered electoral boundaries. The Nationalist Party responded by accepting the role of "Official Opposition" at Stormont, and it soon gave way to such new organizations as the Civil Rights Association and the Social Democratic and Labour Party (SDLP) which emphasized the need for reforms within Northern Ireland rather than the immediate unification of Ireland. Even the early protest marches and riots were related to this process of compromise, focusing as they did on questions of policy reform rather than the maintenance or abolition of the Irish border.

The reform process was not fast enough to satisfy many Catholics, however, and it was much too fast for many Protestants. As the incidence of sectarian violence increased, attention began to turn from questions of social policy to more fundamental issues about the distribution of power. Compromise is much easier in the realm of social policy, where disputes tend to be about degrees of benefit, than it is on constitutional issues which frequently are (or are seen as) zero-sum, win or lose questions. When the distribution of power is at stake, the possibility for compromise is likely to rest with arranging trade-offs on several issues, rather than agreeing upon some intermediate position on each question. In the "national compromise" of 1917 in the Netherlands, for example, the Liberals improved their prospects by obtaining a proportional representation electoral system, the anticlerical Socialists won universal suffrage, and Catholic and Protestant groups were guaranteed public support for religious schools, as Nordlinger has pointed out.

In Ulster during the 1960s it apppeared that Catholics and Protestants might be moving toward just such a compromise; one in which the minority would give allegiance to the United Kingdom in return for political and economic equality with Protestant Ulstermen. In the end, however, neither group would go far enough in this direction to satisfy the other, and elements on each side turned to violence in an attempt to gain one-half of the implied bargain without the other. When Westminster responded to the escalating violence by imposing direct rule, attention turned to other ways of attempting to regulate the conflict. The most obvious of these was the proportionality principle. This principle can be applied to the legislature, as is the case in all countries which have proportional representation electoral systems; to the bureaucracy, as has been true of post-war Austria; and even to the Cabinet, as it did in Lebanon. In 1973 Britain created a new governmental system for Northern Ireland which included a PR-based Assembly and a requirement that both communities be represented in the executive (although in no set proportions). Four months after the new "power-sharing" executive took office, a massive strike by Protestant opponents of the system made the province ungovernable and Britain was forced to revert to direct rule. Some variant of this procedure remained the preference of the SDLP through to the 1980 conference, but no political party which supports such a system has been able to retain the support of a majority of Protestants.

This system also incorporated a third conflict-regulating practice: the mutual veto. Since the executive was required to include representatives of both communities, no action could be taken which was unanimously condemned by either group. With the failure of the power-sharing system, the mutual veto was retained for constitutional matters. Britain insisted that no powers would be transferred to Northern Irish authorities without the consent of both Protestants and Roman Catholics. When the Protestant "loyalist" majority in the Constitutional Convention of 1975-76 recommended the reestablishment of a powerful provincial government based on majority rule, Westminster refused to accept the proposal because it totally lacked support in the minority community. In the discussion paper prepared for the 1980 talks, the British outlined several possibilities. All of these included some sort of mutual veto provision, either through shared executive powers or by means of a system of "weighted" legislative voting.

Purposive depoliticization is the remaining regulatory technique which has been tried in Ulster, although it has been implemented in only limited ways. Even before direct rule a number of contentious policy areas were removed from the political realm by creating appointed bodies to administer such matters as education, health and welfare, and public housing. Direct rule itself can be seen as a massive (if temporary) form of depoliticization since it removes all public policy from the control of competing groups in Northern Ireland. In the longer run the British authorities have determined that control of the policing function, the courts, and electoral laws will not be returned to any Ulster government for the foreseeable future. While these measures reduce the scope of the conflict to some degree, they are not nearly as extensive or effective as the type of depoliticization practiced in Lebanon in the 1950s and Malaysia in the 1960s. In those cases, unlike contemporary Ulster, the leaders of the communal groups tried to avoid making public reference to, or taking governmental action on, issues which were central to the inter-communal conflict. The Alliance Party did attempt to depoliticize sectarian issues in Northern Ireland by explicitly trying to appeal to both Catholics and Protestants, but it won less than 10 percent of the vote in 1973, and again in 1975.

The two techniques which have not been tried in Northern Ireland seem to have been avoided for good reason. There has been no attempt to regulate the conflict by arranging a coalition between the leading political parties in the two communities before elections are held. This sort of arrangement worked reasonably well in Malaysia from the mid-1950s to the end of the 1960s, and in Austria for two decades after the war. It is a variant of Lijphart's consociational model, in which the mass of the conflicting groups have little contact with one another, and an accommodation is worked out at the elite level. Consociationalism seems to work well only in unusually quiescent societies, however, and even in situations in which the public is generally deferential, the freedom of their leaders is unlikely to extend to actions which seem to threaten the vital interests of the group. In Northern Ireland, of course, the conflict between Catholics and Protestants revolves mainly around the question of how legitimate political power is to be distributed. Any attempt at coalition-building would inevitably appear to many Protestants to be an effort to solve the problem by conceding victory to their opponents. From the point of view of many Roman Catholics, the informality of the procedure would mean that their wellbeing depended upon the future goodwill of Protestants to an unacceptable extent.

Neither side has attempted to regulate the conflict by making unilateral concessions, and the justification for avoiding this practice is similar to the objections to the coalition technique. Nordlinger points out that this is the least common of the six practices, for two very good reasons. First of all, if the concessions are made by a party which is not clearly predominant, they are likely to be taken as a sign of weakness and may thus encourage the stronger group to renew its efforts to achieve complete victory. Indeed, there is a large body of literature which suggests that this interpretation may frequently be put on concessions offered by the apparently stronger side. Secondly, of course, extraordinarily strong conciliatory attitudes are required if the more powerful of the conflicting groups is to be motivated to make unilateral concessions. Nordlinger gives the example of the concessions made by the Protestant cantons to the weaker Roman Catholic cantons following the Sonderbund War in Switzerland, but no other case comes to mind. Almost by definition, the goodwill required of the stronger party is unlikely to exist in situations of intense group conflict.

The Mutual Veto

Of the six techniques which Nordlinger found to be successful in other conflicts, then, four have been tried in Ulster, and the remaining two do not seem at all promising. Rather than justifying complete despair, however, I believe that this analysis can help us to identify the limited scope for an initiative that does exist.

The essential clash is between the security concerns of Protestants and those of Catholics. The Protestant community will not accept any proposal which gives executive powers to representatives of the minority. The IRA has made it clear that such an arrangement would not induce it to give up the fight, and Protestants fear that a religiously mixed executive could not combat terrorism with the same determination as a Protestant government. Furthermore, the commitment of the SDLP to the eventual unification of Ireland creates a fear that they would attempt to use the instruments of the state to further this end. From the point of view of Catholics, on the other hand, any system which gives control of the government to the majority creates unacceptable risks. Protestants did use the powers of government to repress the minority from 1921 to 1972, and nothing has happened since direct rule to convince Roman Catholics that a Protestant government would do otherwise in the future.

Given the nature of the conflict, there is no potential compromise which is at all relevant to the central issues, and which the mass publics on either side would accept. Depoliticization is similarly inappropriate since the conflict is about the nature of political institutions rather than their product. The proportionality principle and the mutual veto technique are the only conflict-regulating practices which directly address the question of the distribution of legitimate political authority. Even the proportionality principle misses the heart of the problem, moreover, unless it includes some provision which prevents the majority from overruling the minority. Of Nordlinger's six conflict-regulating practices only the mutual veto is directly relevant to the central issues of the Ulster dispute.

The power-sharing plan provided a direct veto on legislation to both communities by requiring that representatives of each be included in the executive. Either side could stop legislation that it disliked simply by threatening to resign. It has become clear, however, that no Protestant party that supports in which the SDLP is included in the government is likely to be able to maintain its electoral backing. One should note that Brian Faulkner was the most popular politician in Ulster in 1973 and he was the leader of the most powerful party in the province. When he accepted the power-sharing plan, he was forced to resign from the Unionist Party and his personal popularity could not prevent his new Unionist Party of Northern Ireland from becoming an almost irrelevant fringe group. Even William Craig's brief flirtation with the idea of a voluntary coalition during the 1975 Constitutional Convention resulted in his expulsion from the loyalist coalition.

There are other ways in which a mutual veto might be applied however. The British discussion paper for the 1980 talks pointed out that the position of the minority might be protected if some measure of Roman Catholic support was required for the passage of legislation, or for a government to remain in office, even if no Roman Catholics were actually included in the government. The great danger of such a system is legislative deadlock of course, so it might be desirable to make the veto even less direct. Rather than applying to specific bills, or even to the life of a government, the veto might be restricted to the *jurisdiction* of the government. At the moment Westminster has the legal competence to govern all aspects of life in Ulster. The devolution of each specific area of jurisdiction to a Northern Ireland Assembly could be made dependent upon the periodic concurrence of some number of representatives of both communities. In this way a failure to obtain the required agreement would have the effect of simply leaving or returning jurisdiction to Westminster, rather than preventing governmental action altogether.

A great many variations in the details of such a plan are possible. One might start with the requirement of an annual vote on each of the subject areas which Westminster is willing to return to a government of Northern Ireland. For greater safety, the British Secretary of State for Northern Ireland might also be empowered to require such a vote at any time. The more difficult question is how the concurrence of the minority is to be expressed.

The two most obvious solutions are to require separate majorities of Catholic and Protestant members of the Assembly, or to require an extraordinary majority which is so large as to necessitate some measure of Roman Catholic support. There are difficulties with each of these.

The first would require that legislators be classified by religion. While the main Protestant parties have not included any Roman Catholic representatives in the past, both of the parties that did elect Roman Catholics in 1973 and 1975—Alliance and the SDLP—also elected Protestants. In 1975, for example, two of the SDLP's 17 Convention members were Protestants, and two of the eight Alliance members were Roman Catholics. Classification by the religion of individual members would cut across party lines, and would conflict with the claim made by both Alliance and the SDLP to represent political positions rather than sectarian groups. Nor would it be possible to classify members according to the religion of their supporters. In practice it is clear that almost all SDLP ballots are cast by Catholics, as are about half of the votes for Alliance candidates. Short of establishing separate electoral rolls, however, one cannot demonstrate the religious homogeneity of the supporters of any particular candidate. Most of Ulster's large, multi-member constituencies include enough voters of each faith to preclude classification by electoral district.

The requirement of unusually large majorities is a reasonably common feature of the amendment procedures for constitutions, and one could argue that a similar requirement would be appropriate for the establishment and maintenance of the jurisdictional aspects of the constitution of Northern Ireland. The difficulty is that a *very* large majority would have to be required in order to ensure that any Catholic support at all was necessary. Many countries (including Belgium, the Netherlands, Norway and the United States) require a two-thirds vote in their legislatures in order to amend their constitutions, but entirely Protestant unionist parties won 68 percent of the seats in the 1975 Convention. Protestant members of Alliance and the SDLP accounted for a further 10 percent of the membership, so the required level of support would probably have to be as high as 80 percent in order to ensure that success required the vote of even oe Roman Catholic member.

While such a requirement is not inconceivable, it would mean that each of several Protestant parties or coalitions might also possess a veto. In the Convention any group which included more than a quarter of the Protestant members would have been large enough to exercise such a veto. It is one thing to suggest that the Protestant and Catholic communities should each have a veto; it is quite another matter to contemplate giving this power to minority groups within the fractious loyalist alliance.

The concurrent majorities procedure is awkward because members of an assembly who were Roman Catholics would not formally be Catholic representatives, while the special majority procedure faces complications because those who in practice are representatives of Ulster's Catholics are so few in number, even with a proportional representation election system. The best solution might be to take advantage of the British tradition of unwritten constitutional conventions, and simply rely upon the British Secretary of State to determine which party or parties were representative of each religious community at the time of each vote. One could then require the support of a specified proportion of each group—anywhere from a third to a half might be appropriate—or one could also leave the question of what level of support was sufficient to indicate that neither side's wishes were being completely ignored to the judgment of the Secretary of State.

There are at least four clear advantages to this plan. It meets the demand expressed by a majority of Ulstermen that there be no constitutional requirement to put executive powers in the hands of representatives of the minority. Secondly, it does give Catholic representatives the power to prevent the majority from using the institutions of the state to dominate and repress the minority. Thirdly, it creates no danger of complete legislative deadlock; and finally, an unsuccessful attempt to implement such a plan does not seem likely to make things any worse than they are now. Beyond this, this form of mutual veto also has an inherent and desirable dynamic aspect. Its nature is such that it encourages bargaining: we will agree to jurisdiction over this subject in return for that policy. Indeed, it might eventually produce a willingness among Protestants to include some representatives of the Catholic community in the executive. All of the main Protestant parties place great importance on the return of the policing function to a Northern Ireland government, for example, and in the future they might be willing to pay the unavoidable price of a voluntary, bi-confessional coalition.

Conclusion

Of all the techniques for regulating intense conflicts which Nordlinger found in his survey, only the mutual veto procedure directly addresses the central issues of the Ulster dispute. There are variations of this procedure which have not been seriously explored and which might be acceptable both to the political leaders of the province and their followers. The mutual veto suggestion is not new; it was one of several possibilities listed in the paper prepared for the 1980 all-party conference, for example. Why has it not been tried—and why might it be possible to attempt it now?

The answer, I think, is to be found in the British Government's decision to wait for an agreement among the Northern Irish parties to emerge. Both the SDLP and the various Unionist parties have good reasons for not promoting such a plan themselves. On the Protestant side, there is the dismal record of every Unionist leader who has promoted any policy other than the re-establishment of a powerful, majority-rule government: Brian Faulkner losing his party and his followers; William Craig suffering expulsion from the loyalist coalition; Ian Paisley's Democratic Unionist Party (DUP) remaining on the fringe until he gave up the idea of full integration into the United Kingdom. The danger that any initiative will be undercut by competing Protestant factions is too great. For the SDLP there is the hope, however faint, of again taking part in a governing coalition. In 1974 the SDLP became the first political party with roots in the Catholic community ever to be included in a government in the history of Northern Ireland. The leaders of the party may be understandably reluctant to initiate a proposal which would sacrifice their claim to office.

While the proceedings of the talks among the parties during the spring of 1980 have not been made public, the general pattern of the conference is known. The British Government identified a number of central questions, including how the powers of a new government might be exercised "so as to safeguard the interests of the minority community," and each party expressed its views on these issues. Thus Ian Paisley's DUP urged the re-establishment of a system modelled after Westminster, and the SDLP argued for a return to the 1974 power-sharing procedures. The idea of a system based on a mutual veto seems to have escaped serious consideration. Certainly, there was no discussion of a veto which applied to jurisdictional questions, but not directly to normal legislation.

If the British Government were now to propose such a system itself, it might be much more difficult for Ulster's political leaders to continue to demand their own preferred solutions. This plan does not directly contradict any of the basic principles to which the Protestant parties have committed themselves. Their position has changed only slightly since the 1975 Convention elections, at which time the United Ulster Unionist Council demanded that no party be given "a larger share of representation, influence or power than that to which its electoral support entitles it", and that the "Leader of the party with a majority in the House . . .be entrusted to form a government." In so far as the normal legislative process is concerned, both of these conditions would be met. By the end of 1979 political conditions were such that the Official Unionist Party and the Democratic Unionist Party could each realistically hope to be able to either form a government or dominate a governing coalition, should elections be held. The opportunity to hold office might be enough to motivate both parties to accept the veto provisions on jurisdictional matters.

It might be more difficult to obtain SDLP acceptance, since that party has formally committed itself to the establishment of an "administration in which both sections of the community participate to the full," and to the "recognition and acceptance of the Irish Dimension" to Ulster's affairs. Since neither point is incorporated in the mutual veto procedure, SDLP leaders could pursue both their own desire for office and their previously announced principles by rejecting such a plan. They might experience some difficulty in maintaining public support for a negative position if the safeguards of the mutual veto system were widely publicized, and the possibility of eventually bargaining for Cabinet seats would be a countervailing consideration.

None of this should be taken to suggest that there is any certainty that a system of this type could be established, or that it would not collapse shortly after initial acceptance. Indeed, the chances of success are slight at best. Nevertheless, even a slight hope of regulating the terrible battle experienced in Northern Ireland over the last decade is enough to warrant the attempt. While the details may vary considerably from those suggested here, two points do seem clear: the only type of conflict-regulating practice which has even this slight chance of success is one based on the mutual veto; and the only party to the dispute which is at all likely to take such an initiative is the British Government.

THE UNIONISTS[7]

. . .The Unionists of Northern Ireland are justly proud of their heritage and their contribution to the world. As many as eleven American presidents came of their stock. They number field marshals, captains of industry and colonial governors among their great men. They see themselves as a pragmatic, hardheaded, skeptical, robust people, and there is much in their history to justify their view. They have shown a corresponding tendency to regard their nationalist Catholic neighbors throughout the island as a more fanciful and less realistic race, and indeed there may be much in the history of the dispossession and enforced illiteracy of the Catholic community to give color to that view.

History has changed the face and condition of Ireland, and these opinions have been overtaken by events. The south started from a platform of no industry and relatively primitive agriculture in 1921, while the north was the only part of Ireland seriously affected at that time by the Industrial Revolution. Now the south has caught up with and will shortly overtake the north economi-

[7] Excerpt from article entitled "The Irish Question: A British Problem," by John Hume, Leader of the Social Democratic and Labor Party in Northern Ireland. *Foreign Affairs*. 38:304-9. Winter '79. Reprinted by permission of Foreign Affairs, Winter 1979/80. Copyright by the Council on Foreign Relations, Inc., 1979, and the author.

cally. Northern industry is in decline and is for the most part owned by outsiders. The North has no sovereign voice in the world, nor, significantly, in the European Community. Unionists watch with envy tinged with resentment as Dublin, for the second time, exercises the presidency of the Council of the European Community during these months. Unionists are, furthermore, dismayed at the decline of Britain's greatness to a point where, most galling of all, London must now treat Dublin as an equal in the councils of Europe. A hardheaded people should logically draw the conclusion that an arrangement with the south is in its best interest. I have no doubt that they would do so now were the problem of Northern Ireland purely economic. Of course, it is not.

The Unionists are a majority in Northern Ireland, but their political behavior there can only be understood if they are seen, as they feel themselves to be, as a threatened minority on the island of Ireland. Theirs are the politics of the besieged. Hence their stubborn refusal to share power with the minority in Northern Ireland, whom they fear as the Trojan horse of the "real" majority in Ireland, the Catholics. Hence, the similarity between their attitudes and those of the whites of southern Africa.

Can this attitude be unfrozen? There are some grounds for believing that it can. I have mentioned the Sunningdale experiment, the most promising attempt so far to solve the problem. The main Unionist political group at that time, and particularly its leader, the late Mr. Brian Faulkner, showed courage and political agility, and the response of most Unionists to the experiment was by and large benign. The pusillanimity of the Labour government in London, in failing to resist the predictable destructiveness of the demagogues and paramilitaries on the extremes of Unionism, set back the situation almost irremediably; Unionist opinion, it must be admitted, shifted further to the Right as a result, as evidenced by the growing electoral strength of Ian Paisley. Nevertheless, the reality of power-sharing did exist, however tenuously. Unionists, given the right leadership, were seen to be capable of magnanimity. The problem now is to create the conditions where magnanimity can again take hold, this time more securely.

I am also encouraged by what I take to be a resurfacing of traditional Unionist realism. There is a growing suspicion among

Unionists that their dependence on the British guarantee as the sole foundation of their political survival may in the long run be a risky and unprofitable enterprise. No leader of present mainline Unionist opinion has yet found the courage to put this squarely to his people, but several have expressed concern about the trustworthiness of the British.

Now is, as I have suggested, the moment when political leaders in Northern Ireland, in the Republic, and in Britain must radically reexamine their own fundamental assumptions. As I see it, the two greatest problems in Northern Ireland are the British guarantee, which inhibits such reexamination, and the Unionist dependence on it. Given economic developments in the Republic and the growing suspicion about Britain's long-term intentions on the part of many Unionists, this would seem a propitious juncture at which to take a serious initiatve. Only Britain can create the conditions in which Unionists can perceive and pursue their true interests.

I believe that the true interest of Unionists depends precisely on the exercise of their traditional gifts of self-confidence and self-reliance. The time has come for them to believe in themselves as their own best guarantors in a future with the other people of the island of Ireland.

As it is now, Unionists see themselves as a threatened minority on the island of Ireland. If you ask a Unionist how real the threat is, he or she will tell you of friends or relatives who have been murdered or injured by the Provisional IRA. What threat could be more real? That, however, is only a vivid and chilling expression of an even deeper sense of intimidation. Unionists fear that they would be culturally and racially overwhelmed by the Catholic nationalist majority if they were to join with the rest of the island. Would they? This is the challenge to Irish nationalism, to Dublin, to the nationalist minority in Northern Ireland, and to the friends of Irish nationalism around the world.

The campaign of violence of the Provisional IRA has, more than any recent development, set back and distorted the cause of Irish nationalism in the eyes of Unionists, and of British and world opinion. It is clear that a majority of the people in Ireland as a whole, including a majority of Catholics in Northern Ireland, both favor Irish unity as a solution and reject violence as a means of promoting that solution.

The Provisionals have been relatively impervious to the universal rejection of their methods for a number of reasons. First, they are sustained by an extremely simple view of the Irish problem, and in this simplicity they find strength and purpose. For the Provisionals, the Irish problem consists of the British presence in Ireland—nothing more; remove that presence, they claim, and the problem will quickly be solved by the establishment of a unified, independent Irish state. This analysis of things not only affords a simple view of a highly complex situation, but it also provides the inspiration for violent action aimed at inducing British withdrawal. The Provisional reading of the problem also gains from its clear affinities with the vision of the partially successful, and widely revered, insurgents of the 1916-22 period, who, in their determination to secure freedom for the greater part of the Irish people, were understandably distracted from the peculiar circumstances which obtained in the six northeastern counties.

A second factor in Provisional endurance has been the encouragement which they—like the loyalist extremists—have been able to draw from British weakness and prevarication. That weakness has so shown itself not alone in the fact of loyalist intransigence but also in the intermittent British dalliance with Provisional "political spokesmen," whose credentials have been forged by bombs and bullets.

Third, I believe that the case for Irish nationalism has not been clearly enough expounded by Irish nationalist leaders. The Provisionals have not hesitated to exploit the ambiguities of policy and the innuendoes of the public debate to seek to claim support of, or justification for, their actions.

Fourth, unjustifiable excesses by British security forces, condemned by the European Court of Human Rights as inhuman and degrading treatment, created an implacable hostility to Britain in the minds of many who were subjected to them. These excesses, together with the introduction of internment without trial in 1971 (it has since been abandoned), did more to gain recruits for the Provisionals than any exhortations to "blood sacrifice" from the patriarchs of the movement.

Fifth, the absence of political activity from the life of Northern Ireland has provided both an opportunity and an argument to the men of violence: they can with some credibility play upon the frustrations of the minority in the absence of political hope, and they can well ask, in the face of British immobilism: Who but we are doing anything about Northern Ireland?

Finally, it can be seen that the Provisionals have hardened into a ruthless terrorist force which can compensate in terms of experience and technique for what it has lost in political support. It is a long time now since commentators invoked Mao and predicted that, as the water of popular approval dried up, the guerrilla fish would have to abandon the struggle to survive. We can now see that the fish need less water than we had thought. The Provisionals have for several years received only insignificant support from the population of either Northern Ireland or the Republic; yet they retain the ability to disrupt and terrorize.

Indeed, their activities have descended to a level of savagery which has all but numbed the capacity of the public to respond with horror to even their inhuman atrocities. Life has become cheap—and the entire community to some extent dehumanized. "Is there a life before death?" asks a piece of anonymous graffiti on a Belfast wall, with some reason. The writer might also have asked whether there is any childhood left for the battle-scarred children of the ghettos of that city, and of the rest of Northern Ireland.

Aside from the immorality of its actions, the Provisional IRA campaign has no hope of success. It is, I suppose, conceivable that it might eventually frighten a feeble British government out of Northern Ireland before any process could begin. What would undoubtedly follow would be a serious risk of a bloodbath. This would quickly spread to the south, and, after thousands of deaths, would finally resolve itself by the division of the island into two bristling, homogeneous sectarian states, neither stable, both sunk in the obscuratism of their most extreme supporters. No military victory followed by a political settlement is possible in Northern Ireland. That is true not for the Provisionals alone but for the loyalists and the British government as well.

The Irish government and most nationalists in Ireland have repeatedly given convincing evidence of their repudiation of the violence of the Provisionals—the public by its consistent rejection at the polls of those who support violence, and the Irish government by its active pursuit of the men of violence, its commitment of additional police and army units to the border areas, and the introduction of draconian legal measures to secure convictions in the courts. Dublin and Irish opinion generally clearly intend no threat to Unionists; on the contrary, the leaders of Irish-American opinion, which was generally seen by Unionists to be hostile to their interests and indeed supportive of violence, have in recent years repeatedly condemned support for violence from the United States. This has had the double effect of reducing material assistance for the Provisional IRA from the United States and of going some way toward assuaging one source of Unionist anxiety.

Despite these positive elements, there is an important sense in which the principal source of Irish nationalist sentiment, i.e., Dublin, has not yet fully clarified its intentions. Unionists will not be able to bring themselves to entertain seriously the notion of Irish unity unless Dublin unambiguously spells out what it understands by unity and gives clear evidence of its commitments.

The southern state is seen by many Unionists (in varying degrees by the majority) as a lay expression of sectarian Catholic values. As such, it is unacceptable to them. The reality, as I encounter it, is that the Republic is a modern state struggling to develop its economy and society within a European framework. The partition of Ireland, 50 years ago, created a state in the south with an overwhelmingly Catholic population. Inevitably, Catholic values were enshrined in some areas of law, particularly family law, although the state is in other respects one of the least confessional in Europe, with no official church. Unionists have a right to be convinced that the south is serious when it declares its intention to embody pluralist values in the law of the United Ireland to which it aspires. So far, the evidence for these intentions is inadequate.

Even more seriously, those who avow a nationalist solution must clarify how they would implement this. Statements which contain hints of irredentism, of conquest, of compulsion, do not promote a policy of unity; moreover, they give comfort to the men of violence. The Irish government repudiates violence and by its action is seen to do so. It should, nevertheless, in claiming the ground of nationalism, clarify, if necessary *ad nauseam*, its com-

mitment to unity by agreement, only by agreement, and through
reconciliation.

BIBLIOGRAPHY

An asterisk (*) preceding a reference indicates that the article or a part of it has been reprinted in this book.

BOOKS AND PAMPHLETS

Bell, Geoffrey. The Protestants of Ulster. Pluto. '80.

Birrell, Derek and Murie, Alan. Policy and government in Northern Ireland. Barnes & Noble. '80.

Bow, Paul and others. The state in Northern Ireland. St. Martin. '79.

Buckland, Patricia. The factory of grievances. Barnes & Noble. '79.

Buckland, Patricia. A history of Northern Ireland. Holmes & Meier. '81.

Carlton, Charles. Bigotry of blood: documents on the Ulster crisis. Nelson-Hall. '77.

Farell, Michael. Northern Ireland: Orange State. Pluto. '80.

Fields, Rona M. Northern Ireland: society under seige. Transaction. '81.

Fields, Rona M. Society under seige: a psychology of Northern Ireland. Temple. '77.

*FitzGibbon, Constantine. Red Hand: the Ulster colony. Doubleday. '71.

Holland, Jack. Too long a sacrifice: life and death in Northern Ireland since 1969. Dodd. '81

McAllister, Ian. The Northern Ireland Social Democratic and Labour Party: political opposition in a divided sociaty. Holmes & Meier. '78.

McCreary, Alf. Survivors: Documentary account of the victims of Northern Ireland. Beekman. '77.

Meskin, Ken. Northern Ireland: a psychological analysis. Columbia. '80.

Miller, David. Queen's rebels. Ulster loyalism in historical perpective. Barnes & Noble. '78.

O'Dowd, L. et al. Northern Ireland: between civil rights and civil war. Humanities. '81.

Reagan, Ronald. Northern Ireland (President's statement, March 17, 1981). State Dept. Bull. 81: 39. My. '81.

Van Voris, William H. Violence in Ulster: an oral documentary. U. of Mass. Pr. '75.

Winchester, Simon. Northern Ireland in crisis: reporting the Ulster troubles. Holmes & Meier. '75.

PERIODICALS

America. 142:inside cover. F. 9, '80. Of many things. J. A. O'Hare.

American. 143:327-8. N. 22, '80. Refugees from H-block. M. Schwartz.

*America. 143:361. D. 6, '80. Hunger strike on H-block.

America. 144:inside cover. Ap. 25, '81. Of many things. J. H. O'Hare.

America. 145:213. O. 17, '81. Hunger strike ends.

America. 145:234-5. O. 24, '81. Ireland's epidemic of violence. T. P. O'Mahony.

America. 145:inside cover. N. 28, '81. Of many things. R. A. Blake.

America. 147:inside cover. Jl. 24-31, '82. Of many things, J. A. O'Hare.

Business Week. p 46. Jl. 12, '82. Falklands fallout: a blow to peace prospects in Ulster. Dennis Kennedy.

*Christian Century. 98:629-30. Je. 3-10, '81. Northern Ireland's ordeal. Trevor Beeson.

Christianity Today. 26:20-4. Ap. 23, '82. Northern Ireland: Protestantism under siege? A. P. Williamson.

*Commentary. 73:55-64. Ja. '82. Ulster: in the empty house of the stare. Herb Greer.

*Commonweal. 106:228, 237-9. Ap. 27, '79. Northern Ireland under Thatcher. Jack Holland.

*Commonweal. 106:652-4. N. 21, '80. The men on the blanket. Jack Holland.

Commonweal. 108:370-2. Je. 19, '81. What to think about Northern Ireland. D. J. Bowman.

Commonweal. 109:400-1. Jl. 16, '82. Keeping Catholics in their place. D. E. Lowry.

Economist. 281:64-5. N. 14-20, '81. Anglo-Irish eyes are smiling; Orangemen turn purple.

Economist. 281:58+. N. 28-D. 4, '81. Paisley's day.

*Foreign Affairs. 58:300-13. Winter '79. The Irish question: a British problem. John Hume.

Journal of Adolescence. 4:285-94. D. '81. Teenage experiences in a violent society (Northern Ireland). Peter McLachlan.

International Affairs. 58:95-114. Winter '82. Response of the London and Belfast governments to the declaration of the republic of Ireland. Ronan Fanning.

Macleans. 93:4. S. 8, '80. Tragedy of the soul. Brendan Keenan.

Macleans. 93:35-6. N. 17, '80. Hunger that hurts where it counts. Brendan Keenan.

Macleans. 93:26-7. D. 29, '80. When Irish eyes are frowning. Brendan Keenan.

Macleans. 94:18+. Ap. 28, '81. Countryman's lament. Tim Coogan.

Macleans. 94:30. My. 4, '81. Time runs out for Bobby and Ulster. Brendan Keenan.

Macleans. 94:36. My. 11, '81. State of weary expectations. Robert Rodwell.

Macleans. 94:22-3. My. 18, '81. Dublin. London may tremble yet. Brendan Keenan.

Macleans. 94: 21-5. My. 18, '81. Making of a martyr. Carol Kennedy.

Macleans. 94:24. My. 18, '81. Too little and too late. Robert Rod-well.

Macleans. 94:23. Je. 1, '81. Absent persuaders. Brendan Keenan.

Macleans. 94:31-2. N. 30, '81. Ulster's days of rage. Carol Kennedy.

*Nation. 228:300-3. Mr. 24, '79. Town without pity: letters from a Belfast ghetto. Jack Holland.

National Geographic. 159:470-99. Ap. '81. War and peace in Northern Ireland. Bryan Hodgson.

National Review. 32:1471-2. N. 28, '80. Erin go blah. D. K. Mano.

National Review. 33:597. My. 29, '81. Terrible bombast is born.

National Review. 33:656. Je. 12, '81. Reflections on violence. Brian Crozier.

National Review. 33: 1023-5. S. 4, '81. Unsinkable myths. Forrest McDonald.

National Review. 33:1187. O. 16, '81. Irish mess. Brian Crozier.

New Leader. 63:8-9. My. 5, '80. New Ulster initiative. Michael McDowell.

New Leader. 64:8-10. O. 5, '81. Way out in Ulster. J. P. McCarthy.

*New Republic. 183:16-21. N. 15, '80. Troubles today. Jack Beatty.

New Republic. 184:10-12. My. 9, '81. Out of the Maze. Jack Beatty.

New Republic. 184:5-6. My. 23, '81. After Bobby Sands.

New Republic. 185:16-28. O. 14, '81. Belfast's children. Robert Coles.

New Statesman. 102:4. O. 2, '81. Fitzgerald's hollow crusade. Mary Holland.

New Statesman. 102:8. O. 30, '81. Protestants included out. Mary Holland.

New Statesman. 102:14. N. 20, '81. Unity of fear (violence in Northern Ireland). Mary Holland.

New Statesman. 103:6-7. F. 12, '82. Kincoragate puts Paisley on the spot. Andrew Pollack.

*New York Review of Books. 28:2931. O. 22, '81. Hunger strikers. Denis Donoghue.

*New York Times. p 8. N. 7, '81. Leaders of Britain and Ireland to form panel on closer ties. William Borders.

*New York Times. p 10. Mr. 14, '82. Ulster seems headed for a Catholic majority. William Borders.

New York Times Magazine. p 94+. O. 11, '81. Britain's new look at the Irish question. William Borders.

*New York Times Magazine. p 19+. Ag. 2, '81. Ulster's lost generation. John Conroy

*New Yorker. 54:48-50+. My. 8, '78. A reporter at large. Anthony Bailey.

New Yorker. 57:134. Je. 8, '81. Letter from London. Mollie Painter-
   Downs.

Newsweek. 96:24. D. 29, '80. Hunger strike ends. J. Brecher and Lea
   Donosky.

Newsweek. 97:59. Ap. 20, '81. IRA man wins seat in Commons. R. Wil-
   kinson and J. Clifton.

Newsweek. 97:40-1. Death wish in Ulster. B. Levin and Lea Donosky.

Newsweek. 97:38+. My. 11, '81. Ulster's days of rage. B. Levin and Lea
   Donosky.

Newsweek. 97:50-1. My. 18, '81. Legacy of Bobby Sands. B. Levin and
   others.

Newsweek. 97:59. My. 25, '81. Politics of suicide. P. Webb and T. Clifton.

Newsweek. 97:53. Je. 1, '81. Split in British ranks. S. Strasser and T.
   Clifton.

Newsweek. 97:51-2. Je. 15, '81. Election with a difference. John Brecher
   and Lea Donosky.

Newsweek. 98:36. Jl. 20, '81. Mediation effort collapses.

Newsweek. 98:38. Ag. 17, '81. Inside the Maze prison. Lea Donosky.

Newsweek. 98:56. O. 12, '81. IRA strikers end their fast.

Newsweek. 98:77. O. 19, '81. Family matter. P. Webb and Lea Donosky.

Newsweek. 98:58. N. 30, '81. Protestant days of rage. J. Le Moyne and
   S. Mydans.

Newsweek. 99:10. Je. 21, '82. Maze Prison: more trouble is brewing. Eileen Keerdoja.

Newsweek. 100:31-2. Ag. 2, '82. The IRA's return to terror. John Brecher.

*Political Quarterly. p 451-63. O./D. '80. Regulating conflicts: The case
   of Ulster. Terrance G. Carroll.

Reader's Digest. 120:91-5. Ja. '82. Northern Ireland's agony without
   end. David Reed.

Rolling Stone. p 14-19. Je. 25, '81. Ireland agonistes. Warren Hinckle.

Time. 116:28. Jl. 14, '80. New plans for sharing power.

Time. 116:48. D. 15, '80. Hunger strike in H-block.

*Time. 116:39. D. 28, '80. End to a dangerous fast.

Time. 117:32. F. 23, '81. Call to arms.

Time. 117:32-5. My. 4, '81. Deathwatch in H-block. George Russell and
   others.

Time. 117:35. My. 4, '81. Making of a martyr. J. D. Palmer and others.

Time. 117:34. My. 11, '81. Bracing for a blowup. George Russell and
   others.

Time. 117:52-4. My. 18, '81. Shadow of a gunman. George Russell and
   others.

Time. 117:36. Je. 1, '81. Death cycle.

Time. 118:43. Ag. 3, '81. Disaffection.

*Time. 118:46-8. Ag. 17, '81. Ready to die in the Maze. Robert Ajemian.

Time. 118:32. S. 21, '81. Uneasy calm.

*Time. 118:58. 0. 12, '81. The strike ends.

Time. 118:58. N. 30, '81. Edging toward the abyss. G. D. Garcia and others.

Time. 118:44. D. 7, '81. Unleashing the third force.

Time. 119:33-7. Ja. 11, '82. Belfast. Roger Rosenblatt.

Time. 120:22-3. Ag. 2, '82. Terror on a summer's day (IRA's bomb attack on the Queen's Household Cavalry). Russ Hoyle.

U.S. News & World Report. 90:61-2. F. 2, '81. In Ulster, violence turns hope to despair. Robert Haeger.

U.S. News & World Report. 90:34. My. 11, '81. Prisoner's fast lights a fuse in tortured Ulster. Stewart Powell.

U.S. News & World Report. 90:35-6. My. 18, '81. For Ulster, despair shrouds the future. Stewart Powell.

U.S. News & World Report. 93:7. Ag. 2, '82. Bloodshed and bumbling in Britain.

*Washington Post. Ja. 8, '82. If you had given me a visa. . . .Ian Paisley.